Babbo Roberto & Mamma Silvia 1984

Nonni, Romolo & Marisa 1979

Maria Rachele & Mattia 1993

Maria, Mamma Silvia, Angela, 1965

Eli, Giovanni, Simone con Roberto 1985

SI MANGIA

RECIPES: MATTIA RISALITI • PHOTOS: NATHALIE MOHADJER • DESIGN & STYLING: MILIA SEYPPEL

SI MANGIA

PRESTEL

MUNICH • LONDON • NEW YORK

INDICE

CONTENTS

LUNCH WITH THE FAMILY

An intimate chamber play—that's the best analogy I can come up with for lunch at our place. Our family get-togethers are a real drama, every single time. There are 46 of us all together, and our communal meals regularly involve around 30 people. The massive table in the garden then becomes the centrepiece of the whole affair. This offers plenty of space for all the protagonists, so everyone can take a seat and become part of the spectacle.

The performance kicks off with the arrival of the children. The opening scene features little Gemma, proudly showing me her dress and then waiting expectantly for me to admire her gorgeous shoes. Her pastel footwear reflects the colours of this lovely sunny day.

Slowly, the garden fills with people. Giacomo and Noemi are already here with

their four kids. Stefano and Silvia arrive with three more little guests. The bright sounds of children's voices mingle with the distant, deep chimes of the church bell. Now Maria Rachele and Lorenzo are here too with their own sonorous quartet of Giuditta, Vittorio, Francesco, and Emma. Then there are my parents, of course, plus the two of us with little Elio.

Everyone gathers around the long table. Noisy greetings and kisses are exchanged as everyone finds a seat. The colourful, densely woven tablecloth dates back years and has been laid with Italian porcelain. Antipasti are already plated up and waiting to be eaten. The stage is perfectly set.

A brief moment of reflection is followed by the toast, then the first act begins with the primo: penne al sugo. It's time to eat!

The meal is accompanied by loud laughter, the clink of cutlery on porcelain, jovial snippets of conversation, and even some singing.

From the head of the table, I can already spy the second course, held up high above the heads of the junior performers as they put on a wild theatre show from their seats. Slices of brilliant yellow lemons are draped around the main course. Today we are eating the ultimate dish: roast chicken with patate arrosto, plenty of salad, and a lemon and rosemary garnish. The assembled company applauds, and plates are immediately held out for the star of the show.

Now comes the dramatic climax: tasting the feast on offer. Words and gestures combine in a sublime dramatic composition.

Plates are emptied and there is loud talking and laughter. The more junior "extras" have already slipped away from the table to carry on their cheerful racket elsewhere in the garden.

The final act. My mother emerges from the kitchen with a pot of coffee. But the finest theatre prop is yet to appear: the cake. An appreciative murmur ripples through the group. This is the finale we have all been waiting for.

Afterwards, we linger for hours at the table as the afternoon fades away and blends into early evening. The participants express their thanks for the exquisite meal and leave the stage. Slowly, ever so slowly, the curtain falls on proceedings.

Caro Mattia,

I think your passion for cooking began when you went to Berlin. Enjoying great food together was your way of expressing affection! In other words, your love of meeting people prompted you to lay the table and pamper others with your cooking, encouraging intimacy and building connections.

When it comes to getting to know someone, your tried and tested method is to cook and enjoy food together in a welcoming environment.

All my children are incredibly different. It's impossible to say how or why the 11 of you turned out the way you have (even if your granny Marisa is forever seeking out similarities between you).

In family photos, you occupy a central position between your siblings. Five on the right and five on the left, with you, Mattia, seated plumb in the middle. Your place in the family has helped you stay connected to everyone, always trying to build bridges between people by bringing them together.

Even now that you're a married man with your own family, we are constantly amazed at the way you seize the chance to learn new things. This desire to learn is like a thirst for innovation. And an appreciation of food is your creative outlet (no wonder we say that the way to someone's heart is through their stomach). It's a fundamental part of your personality.

As we say in Italian: "At the table, nobody grows old." That's because good food makes an unforgettable impression, evoking the past as if it were timeless and of the moment. No doubt the echo of your Italian home inspired your desire "to speak and why not also sing" through stories, culture, flavours, colours, and shapes, which you then lovingly interpret to share with your Berlin friends at the dinner table.

Your Mamma Silvia

INTRODUCTION

It isn't hard to cook great food in Tuscany. For one thing, the ingredients are so good, you don't really need to do much to conjure up a delicious meal. Tuscan cuisine is also known as *cucina povera* (meaning "poor kitchen"), which refers principally to cooking done by ordinary people, using inexpensive ingredients where nothing at all is wasted. But the term also describes the ability to produce fabulous meals with simple resources. All you have to do is throw two or three things in a pan, and the result is delicious. There is nothing particularly elaborate about our food—in Tuscany, our ideal mealtime companions are a slice of bread and a close friend. The main purpose is spending time together. Eating is not just about nutritional intake; it's about being together. Food is a social event, wherever we are. Even when travelling with friends and renting a cabin in beautiful natural surroundings, food and drink are things to be enjoyed together.

In Tuscany we have a huge variety of culinary options in relatively close proximity, all offering delicious dishes that vary slightly from place to place. We think nothing of driving for an hour just for an afternoon snack, setting off somewhere to get a particular item that we have set our heart on eating and that can't be found elsewhere, whether it's a panini with first-rate mortadella or arista with egg. It's all about having a tale to tell about where you ate, and convincing yourself that nowhere else would have provided such delicious food. The food itself becomes a topic of discussion while we are eating.

I am one of 11 siblings, and communal meals have always been an essential part of our family's social life. When we were children, at 8 pm a shout would resonate around the house: "Si mangia!" ("we're eating"). That meant it was time for supper, and everyone would drop everything, whatever

they might be doing. The evening meal took a lot of organising because there were so many of us: 11 children between the ages of 1 and 20. We cooked together, helped my mother, laid the table, cleared away afterwards, and looked after our younger brothers and sisters. There was always plenty to do, every single day. Eating together as a family was non-negotiable. We would talk, laugh, and enjoy the food. Nothing has changed today, even though we no longer live at home with my parents. One of us is always there on a daily basis, usually several of us, and my mother, my father, or one of their children will cook for each other and eat together.

When I moved to Berlin 10 years ago, I wanted to experience something new, a different culture. That was the moment I became aware of the benefits of my home. I enjoyed Berlin and the culinary world it revealed to me, with all the different nationalities and dishes that I had never encountered before, but at the same time it whetted my appetite for home. I cooked recipes I had grown up with to remind me of my roots and to share my culture with my new friends. Cooking for other people started as a hobby, turned into a passion, and then became my job.

Professionally—but also privately—I've always been interested in visiting regional producers and understanding their craft to experience the quality of the produce. When buying ingredients, I try to seek out carefully chosen shops and businesses, and I use the supermarket as little as possible. Italy has lots of family-run businesses producing or selling food. These form the foundation of Italian food culture, which is why they are held in such high esteem. The stories and the people who produce our food are just as important to me as the products themselves.

LA POGGIANELLA

My grandmother (nonna) Marisa's house (which she acquired in the 1970s) was "our" place and the venue for family get-togethers. In the Carmignano hills, surrounded by olive trees and vineyards, we celebrate, spend days and evenings together, talk, laugh, and enjoy the cool breeze that wafts here on hot summer days (sadly, not always).

When I say "we," I mean my siblings, Giovanni, Simone, Elisabetta, Giacomo, Maria Rachele, Stefano, Giuditta, Ester, Francesco, and Tommaso; my parents, Roberto and Silvia; and all our partners and kids, of course. Every year at Christmas and Easter we are at least 40 people. On these occasions, Poggianella is the only place where we can all fit round a table (at least the adults). In summer we regularly spend Sundays together, baking pizzas in the wood-fired oven and cooking in the kitchen, setting up long tables on the patio to sit and pass the time together.

The photos for this book were taken here. It is somewhere we love spending time, a place associated with so many shared memories, where we make the most of every possible moment to be together.

ANTIPASTI

&

CONTORNI

STARTERS AND SIDES

L'AGRICOLTORE

When I am out in the garden at Poggianella, every so often I hear a loud rattling: it's Edoardo Pratesi driving his tractor past our garden gate to work on the neighbouring vineyard. All the land next to our house is cultivated by this young farmer. Edoardo produces a typical vin santo, a sweet, regional dessert wine that I use in my recipe for Crostini di Fegatini (p. 28).

Further up from our house are his olive trees, which are harvested along with the trees on our property and in the neighbourhood to produce virgin olive oil. The olives that Edoardo uses for his oil are called Frantoiano, Leccino, and Moraiolo, and they only grow in Tuscany. The oil has a distinctive, robust flavour and is excellent for making salads. In Tuscany, we place a great emphasis on the quality of ingredients, and olive oil plays a key role because it is used in so many different ways. We always have a bottle of Edoardo's oil at home.

Edoardo also produces the renowned fichi di Carmignano, dried figs with a slight hint of aniseed, made according to a traditional Carmignano recipe. All his products are organic and are distributed under the Pieve dei Medici label. More information can be found at www.pievedeimedici.com.

ACCIUGHE ALLA POVERA

PICKLED ANCHOVIES ON BREAD

The first time I ate acciughe alla povera (poor man's anchovies) was when my siblings Giovanni, Elisabetta, Simone, and I visited the parents of my sister-in-law Maddalena at their holiday home on the island of Elba. Her parents had prepared five kilos (11 pounds) of acciughe for us. However, they hadn't calculated that four members of the Risaliti family would easily pack away double that amount. We wolfed down all of the acciughe alla povera and almost the same weight of bread in less than 15 minutes. I was blown away by this dish.

Serves 4
Preparation: 30 min
Time to make in advance: 8 hrs

INGREDIENTS
For the anchovy fillets:
400 g (14 oz) fresh
anchovies
250 ml (1 cup) white
wine vinegar
500 ml (2 cups) water
1 kg (2.2 lbs) Tropea
red onions
1 small fresh red chilli
Salt
4 tbsp extra-virgin olive oil

For the bread:
4 slices of toast
Butter
Juice of 1 lemon
Salt
Freshly ground black pepper

Also: 1 bowl with ice cubes

PREPARATION
Wash the anchovies carefully under running water.

To gut the anchovies: Hold each anchovy belly-upward in the palm of one hand and grasp the gills and mouth with your index finger and thumb. Poke the index finger of your other hand through the belly just below the mouth, and gently run it down the fish to the tail, pulling out the innards.

To fillet the anchovies: Run your thumb along the spine of the fish, then fold the fish open. The central bone should now be exposed. Carefully pull out the central bone from tail to head. The head and tail of the fish should come away from the fillet as you do this.

Rinse the anchovy fillets under running water and transfer to a bowl of iced water. After 2 minutes, remove them from the water, pat them dry, and place them in a clean bowl. Cover with the white wine vinegar and 1 tablespoon of water. Leave the anchovies to rest in the fridge for 4–6 hours.

At the end of this chilling time, the anchovies will be "cooked;" because they were submerged in vinegar, they will have taken on a darker colour and be hard and firm. Drain well to completely remove the vinegar.

Thinly slice the Tropea onions. Finely chop the chilli. Place the anchovy fillets slightly overlapping in a bowl so that the base is covered. Season lightly with salt, then add the chopped chilli and a few onion slices. Cover with another layer of anchovies, then onion rings, and so on until everything has been used. Cover with the olive oil. The oil preserves the freshness and flavour of the anchovies. Season to taste with salt and pepper.

Leave the anchovies to rest at room temperature for at least 2 hours before serving to allow the full flavour of the dish to develop. Then, liberally spread the toast slices with butter, top each one with fish fillets, lemon juice, and some salt and pepper, and enjoy.

ZONZELLE PROSCIUTTO E STRACCIATELLA
PIZZA DOUGH BALLS WITH PROSCIUTTO AND STRACCIATELLA CHEESE

There are lots of names for this dish: in Romagna they are known as ficattole, in Florence they are coccoli, in Prato the residents call them zonzelle. If we have any leftover dough, for example after making pizzas, we use it to make these delicious dough balls. My brother Giacomo always loved kneading the dough. He would say to our mother, "Mamma, impasto io, mi faccio i muscoli!" ("Mum, let me do the kneading, it's good for my muscles!") Kneading dough was a body-building workout for him!

Nowadays we use a food processor, but we still keep a bit of dough back when we are cooking pizza so we can make zonzelle the following day.

My favourite way to eat zonzelle is to split them open while still warm. Then, I put a little spoonful of stracciatella cheese and a slice of prosciutto crudo on each half for a delicious, quick snack.

Serves 6
Preparation: 10 min
Resting time: 90 min
in the fridge
Cooking time: 20 min

INGREDIENTS
For the dough:
15 g (0.5 oz) fresh brewer's yeast
1 tsp sugar
400 g (3¼ cups) plain
(all-purpose) flour
Salt
150 ml (⅔ cup) lukewarm water
150 ml (⅔ cup) lager beer

For frying:
2 litres (8½ cups) groundnut oil

To serve:
100 g (3.5 oz) thinly sliced
prosciutto crudo
300 g (10 oz) stracciatella cheese

PREPARATION
Put the fresh brewer's yeast and sugar in a small bowl and mash with a fork until well combined, ensuring the yeast has disintegrated. Add the flour and a pinch of salt to the mashed yeast and combine well.

Transfer this mixture to a shallow bowl, slowly add the lukewarm water and beer, and stir with a spatula until you have a sticky dough. Cover the bowl and leave the dough to prove for about 90 minutes in the fridge.

Heat the groundnut oil to 180°C/350°F. Fetch the dough from the fridge, divide it into portions using two spoons, and fry the zonzelle in the groundnut oil. As soon as the zonzelle are nicely browned, drain them on kitchen paper, then transfer to a plate and season with a pinch of salt. Serve with the prosciutto and stracciatella cheese.

CROSTINI DI FEGATINI ALLA TOSCANA
TOAST WITH CHICKEN LIVER PÂTÉ

At home in Italy, we usually eat three courses at lunchtime: a starter (antipasto), a main course (primo), and a second course (secondo). Crostini are a classic starter and an essential Tuscan dish that naturally had to be included in this cookbook. In our family, this savoury pâté on crusty bread is served whatever the occasion: for birthdays, at Christmas, or as part of an ordinary lunch.

Recipes for this dish are ten a penny, but the most important components are capers and anchovies. For deglazing the liver, I use vin santo from Carmignano, which gives the whole dish a special flavour. If that is not available, you can also use red wine. Opinions vary when it comes to the consistency of the pâté—some like it smooth, others prefer more texture—and the type of bread it should be served with. My nonna Tina always used thick slices of white bread, similar to a sliced baguette, while my nonna Zita preferred a thinly sliced loaf. These days, I serve this pâté on sourdough bread, but the main things to ensure are that the liver is beautifully creamy and the bread is toasted.

Serves 4
Preparation: 30 min
Cooking time: 30 min

INGREDIENTS
20 ml (1.5 tbsp) extra-virgin olive oil
60 g (4 tbsp plus 1 tsp) butter
1 white onion, chopped
100 g (3.5 oz) chicken hearts, rinsed and drained
300 g (10 oz) chicken livers, rinsed and drained
3 or 4 sage leaves
150 ml (½ cup) vin santo (Italian dessert wine)
300 ml (1¼ cup) chicken stock
50 g (1.75 oz) capers
2–3 tinned, oil-packed anchovy fillets, drained
1 tsp tomato concentrate (paste)
Salt
Freshly ground black pepper

For serving:
4 thick bread slices, toasted
115 ml (½ cup) chicken stock, warmed
Capers

PREPARATION
Heat the oil and butter in a medium pan. Add the chopped onion and sauté until golden brown.

Next, add the chicken hearts and livers and the sage and braise until all the liquid has evaporated. Deglaze the pan with the vin santo, add the tomato concentrate, then simmer for 15 to 20 minutes, gradually adding the chicken stock as the chicken hearts and livers cook.

Make sure the sauce is neither too dry nor too runny, but has a spreadable consistency. At the end of the cooking time, add the capers and anchovies, then season to taste with salt and pepper. The cooked chicken livers and hearts can now be chopped into small or large chunks as preferred. The right proportion of liver and chicken hearts is important. The slight bitterness of the liver becomes milder when enough chicken hearts are added, giving the liver pâté a deeper and rounder flavour.

To serve: Dunk the toast briefly into the stock. While the pâté is still warm, spread it on the toast and garnish each serving with a few capers.

BIETOLE PEPERONCINO E ACCIUGHE
SWISS CHARD WITH CHILLI AND ANCHOVIES

One of our most popular side dishes is bietole (Swiss chard). This ingredient can be found everywhere in Tuscany, sometimes even already cooked and pre-packed. I've added a slight twist to this recipe by including chilli and anchovies, which complement the sweetness of the vegetable beautifully.

Bietole goes well with lots of dishes. For example, it makes an excellent accompaniment for a roast, but it can also be served with fish or even with other side dishes. It doesn't take long to make and is absolutely delicious.

Serves 4
Preparation: 15 min
Cooking time: 20 min

INGREDIENTS

1 kg (2 lbs) Swiss chard
(with stems)
2 tbsp extra-virgin olive oil
2 garlic cloves
1 fresh red chilli
6 tinned anchovy fillets, drained
Zest and juice of 1 lemon
Salt

Also:
ice cubes

PREPARATION

Wash the Swiss chard thoroughly and trim off the lower section of the stalks. Peel the remaining stalks on both sides using a knife or peeler.

Fill a saucepan with water. Add the Swiss chard vertically to the pan so that the leaves stick up out of the water and just the stalk is covered. Cook for about 10 minutes at medium heat, slowly pressing the leafy section downwards as the stalk gradually softens. Continue cooking, uncovered, for another 5 minutes. Meanwhile, fill a large bowl with ice water.

Immediately drain the Swiss chard and immerse it in the ice water to stop it from cooking any further. Drain and set aside.

Heat the oil in a small pan and briefly sauté the chilli and 2 anchovies for about 5 minutes, breaking down the anchovies with a wooden spoon.

To serve, place the Swiss chard on a dish and pour the chilli and anchovy oil over top. Drizzle with the lemon juice, garnish with the lemon zest and remaining anchovies, and season with salt.

SUGO AL POMODORO O POMAROLA

HOMEMADE TOMATO SAUCE

Sugo al pomodoro (which translates simply to "tomato sauce") is far more than a mere sauce. Sugo al pomodoro is one of the most fundamental components in Italian cuisine. It is an essential building block for numerous dishes, and there are lots of recipes and different variations for making it. My mother always cooks a bit extra and keeps some of the sauce in the fridge to make various other dishes. Many of my own recipes also rely on sugo al pomodoro (or sugo, for short)— for example, Polpette al Pomodoro, (p. 102), Parmigiana (p. 88), Crespelle alla Fiorentina (p. 75), and Topini al Pomodoro (p. 76). But you can just eat it on its own with some pasta. My mother likes to tell the story of when my sister Ester was pregnant and spent nine months craving pasta with sugo al pomodoro.

Serves 4
Preparation: 30 min
Cooking time: 60 min

INGREDIENTS

2 kg (4½ lbs) fresh Canestrino
or San Marzano tomatoes
Salt
1 carrot
½ white onion
1 tbsp extra-virgin olive oil
4 sprigs basil

PREPARATION

Carefully wash the tomatoes and remove the stems. Slice each tomato in half lengthwise and use a spoon to remove the central section containing the seeds. Place the halved tomatoes in large saucepan and cook gently over a low heat for about 30 minutes, turning them occasionally.

When the tomatoes are soft, season with salt. Turn the tomatoes carefully and let them cook for a few more minutes. Gradually process the tomatoes with a Mouli rotary grater (small to medium holes), catching the purée in a bowl. (Alternatively, press the tomatoes through a sieve into a bowl to make the purée.)

Finely dice the carrot and onion.

Add the oil to the same pan you used to cook the tomatoes, then add the chopped onion and carrot. Sauté for 5–6 minutes, stirring occasionally. Stir in the puréed tomatoes and cook over low heat for a few more minutes, stirring occasionally.

Check that the sugo has the desired creamy consistency, decant it into a container, add the basil leaves, and use it for whatever dish you fancy.

CARCIOFI AFFOGATI ALLA ROMANA
ROMAN-STYLE DROWNED ARTICHOKES

Artichokes are an exceptionally popular vegetable in Italy. They are harvested in spring and autumn and form the basis for lots of very different dishes. I have tried out all sorts of recipes using artichokes, and this one—even if it isn't typical of Tuscany—is one of my favourites.

Whenever I'm making carciofi affogati, I'm reminded of a funny thing my father once said. He was in Austria (where he lived for a number of years), and when serving a pan of artichokes, he got the German word for artichokes (artischocken) muddled up with the German word for old socks (alte socken), announcing his dish in broken German to his friends as: "Here are some old socks."

I use lots of olive oil in this dish to give the stuffed artichokes a unique taste. The artichokes really absorb the flavour of the oil. The filling, combined with sweet artichokes and olive oil, is so delicious that it really is worth preparing several artichokes at once. They work beautifully as a side dish for a roast or as a starter.

Makes 10
Preparation: 20 min
Cooking time: 30–35 min

INGREDIENTS
Zest and juice of 1 lemon
10 artichokes
1 large bunch parsley, finely chopped
4 garlic cloves, minced
200 ml (1 cup) extra-virgin olive oil
Salt
Freshly ground black pepper

TIP
Use gloves when cleaning the artichokes to protect your hands and nails from turning black.

PREPARATION
Fill a large, shallow bowl with water and add the lemon juice (the bowl should be big enough to accommodate all the prepared artichokes).

Next, prepare the artichokes: Remove the hard outer green leaves from the artichokes to reveal the pale-yellow leaves around the heart. Discard the leaves you have removed. Peel and trim the stalks so that, later on, you can stand up all the artichokes alongside each other in a saucepan. Add the trimmed remnants from the stalks to the lemon water. Scrape out the hairs from the centre of the artichokes using a teaspoon. Put the prepared artichokes in the lemon water to prevent them from discolouring.

Remove the trimmed stalk remnants from the water, chop them finely, and combine them with the parsley, garlic, lemon zest, and salt and pepper to taste in a medium bowl. Carefully open each artichoke as if it were a flower, and stuff it with the parsley mix.

Transfer the stuffed artichokes to a large, wide saucepan, positioning them vertically next to each other with the stalks pointing up. Drizzle with extra virgin olive oil and pour in sufficient water to cover the artichoke hearts but leave the stalks pointing up above the surface.

Simmer over the lowest heat with a lid on for about 25–30 minutes, until the artichokes are soft. At the end of the cooking time, leave the artichokes in the covered pan for 10 minutes to rest. Serve warm.

TONNO DEL CHIANTI
FAKE TUNA FROM CHIANTI

Tonno del Chianti means "tuna from Chianti"—the only thing is, the Chianti region is in inland Tuscany where there are no fish. Instead, the locals have created their own deceptively genuine alternative to tuna. This preserved pork has a similar consistency and appearance to tuna fish. Rather than a substitute, this is a wonderful dish in its own right with its own distinct flavour. It tastes excellent on a slice of bread. It also keeps for a while preserved in oil and can be served as an antipasto or a snack between meals.

Serves 4
Preparation: 20 min, plus 45 min after preserving
Time to make in advance:
4–5 days
Cooking time: 5 hrs

INGREDIENTS
1 kg (2 lbs) pork loin
200 g (7 oz) coarse salt
2 sprigs rosemary

For the stock:
1 litre (4¼ cups) white wine
1 litre (4¼ cups) water
2 bay leaves
2 sprigs rosemary
Whole black peppercorns
1 tsp juniper berries

For the preserving jar:
5 bay leaves
Whole black peppercorns
Plenty of sunflower seed oil

TIP
For a very tender and delicate texture, I recommend using pork loin or alternatively shoulder or leg. Chianti tuna goes wonderfully with a salad made from cooked cannellini beans, freshly chopped spring onions, and a splash of Tuscan virgin olive oil.

PREPARATION

To marinate the pork: Remove any tendons and fat from the meat and slice it into roughly 2-cm/¾-in-thick pieces. Place the pieces of meat in a sealable container, layering them up and sprinkling each layer with coarse salt. Add a final sprinkling of salt and top with the sprigs of rosemary. Seal the container and refrigerate for 3–4 days.

Rinse the salt off the meat under cool running water.

To make the stock: Pour the wine and water into a medium pot and bring to a boil.

When the wine solution begins to bubble, add the bay leaves, rosemary, a few peppercorns, the juniper berries, and the meat. Cover with a lid, reduce the heat to low, and simmer for 4–5 hours.

At the end of the cooking time, turn off the heat and leave the meat to cool completely in the cooking liquid. Then, drain the meat and use your hands to split the pieces into small chunks.

Transfer these pieces of meat to a couple of clean, sterilised screw-top jars. Add a few bay leaves and peppercorns, then cover liberally with sunflower seed oil and seal.

The meat will keep in the fridge for at least 1 month. Remove from the refrigerator a couple of hours before serving.

POMODORI INFINITI DELLA NONNA MARISA
NONNA MARISA'S INFINITE ROASTED TOMATOES

After a visit to Nonna Marisa, she would often give us a tray of pomodori al forno to take home with us. This consisted of many layers of tomatoes, separated with baking paper. When we ate the tomatoes, it seemed as though they were never-ending, as one layer concealed another beneath it. So, we named this dish Pomodori Infiniti della Nonna Marisa—Nonna Marisa's infinite roasted tomatoes. As kids, we liked these tomatoes best when they were served cold the following day straight from the fridge.

Tomatoes were initially introduced to Europe in the early 16th century. Italy was the first country where tomatoes were actually consumed rather than just being used as a culinary decoration. The people of Tuscany were fond of experimentation and soon adapted their menu to include foods from the "New World," such as potatoes, corn, bell peppers, and beans. These days, it is impossible to imagine Italy without tomatoes; they are an essential ingredient in traditional Italian cuisine.

Serves 4
Preparation: 30 min
Roasting time: 30 min

INGREDIENTS
80 g (1.75 lbs) medium
ripe tomatoes

For the filling:
100 g (3.5 oz) breadcrumbs
60 g (2 oz) grated Parmesan
8 basil leaves, finely chopped
3 garlic cloves, grated
2 tbsp extra-virgin olive oil
Salt
Freshly ground black pepper
Dried chilli flakes (optional)

PREPARATION
Preheat the oven to 180°C/350°F (non-fan setting). Line a baking tray with baking paper.

Wash the tomatoes, cut them in half, and remove the core and seeds. Use a spoon to scoop the flesh into a large bowl. (Set the hollowed-out tomatoes aside.) Then, transfer the flesh to a cutting board and chop it finely with a knife.

Return the chopped tomato flesh to the bowl, add the breadcrumbs, Parmesan, basil, garlic, and olive oil, and toss to combine. Season with salt and pepper and the optional chopped chilli. Stir everything together until you have a loosely combined mixture. If it seems too damp, add some more breadcrumbs.

Scoop the mixture into the hollowed-out tomatoes and transfer these to the prepared baking tray. Drizzle with olive oil and bake for about 30 minutes, until the breadcrumbs are golden.

Remove the roasted tomatoes from the oven and leave them to rest for 10–15 minutes; serve lukewarm.

CROSTINO AL LARDO DI COLONNATA

TOAST WITH LARDO

Crostini, little slices of toast with toppings, are a popular antipasto in Tuscany (for example Crostini di Fegatini, p. 28). These might be served at all sorts of special events or ordered as an appetizer with a pre-dinner drink.

Crostino al lardo is made using a slightly larger slice of bread that is topped with exquisite, long-cured pork back. Lardo di Colonnata is named after the little hamlet of Colonnata in the mountains of Tuscany. Marble is quarried here, and this pork has always been a nourishing meal for the hard-working miners.

Serves 4
Preparation: 10 min
Baking time: 10 min

INGREDIENTS
5 thin slices white bread
10 thin slices lardo di Colonnata
Freshly ground black pepper
Fine sea salt
Leaves from 1 sprig fresh
rosemary, finely chopped

PREPARATION
Preheat the oven to 200°C/400°F (grill setting).

Place two thin slices of lardo on each slice of bread. Arrange the bread on a lined baking tray and grill in the preheated oven for about 5 minutes, until the lardo begins to melt and the bread turns golden brown.

Season the lardo-topped crostini with freshly ground pepper and salt, then sprinkle with the rosemary. Serve and eat immediately.

ARANCE CONDITE
SPICED ORANGES

My mother once told me about the first time she saw a spiced orange when she was 11 years old and visiting her nonna Zita. She didn't want to eat it back then and thought it was strange to eat salted fruit. Nonna Zita ate spiced oranges very frequently, especially when her stomach was bothering her. Years later, as a grown woman, my mother tried spiced oranges for the first time at her aunt Ada and uncle Brunero's house. From that day onward, these oranges made a regular appearance on our table, too. The spiced orange, according to my poetic mother, has become an "appetising interlude," a "joyous side dish." Quick to make and with a sweet and savoury flavour, this is a perfect, refreshing companion for other food. This dish is so ingenious and simple, we eat it on a regular basis both in summer and winter.

Serves 6
Preparation: 20 min

INGREDIENTS

1 tbsp fennel seeds
3 whole black peppercorns
3 tbsp extra-virgin olive oil
1 kg (2 lbs) oranges
300 g (10 oz) grapefruit
1 tbsp red wine vinegar
Fine sea salt
10 mint leaves

PREPARATION

Toast the fennel seeds and peppercorns in a small pan over a moderate heat until they release their essential oils, then crush them roughly with a mortar and pestle. Put the crushed spices back in the pan, add the olive oil, and put the pan over moderate heat. As soon as the first little bubbles appear, remove the pan from the heat and let it stand until the oil is at room temperature.

Prepare each orange by slicing away the top and bottom to reveal the flesh of the fruit. Place the flat base on a chopping board, and use a knife to cut away the peel from top to bottom, making sure you completely remove the white pith, which has a bitter flavour. Finally, slice the oranges into rounds.

Remove the peel from the grapefruit in the same way as just described. Instead of slicing the grapefruit, though, separate the segments by cutting between the dividing membranes with a knife. Set the segments aside.

Squeeze the juice from what is left of the fruit into a small bowl. Add the fennel oil and red wine vinegar to the bowl with the reserved grapefruit juice, season with salt, and use a fork to whisk the ingredients into an emulsion.

Arrange the sliced oranges and grapefruit segments on a large plate. Drizzle the fruit with the fennel oil dressing. Garnish with mint leaves to serve.

FIORI FRITTI RIPIENI

FRIED STUFFED COURGETTE FLOWERS

I am still fascinated by the idea that fiori fritti involves eating the flowers from a vegetable. There is something very special about the shape—and of course the taste—of these flowers, not least because you can only eat this dish in summer. In Italy, the tradition is to fry the flowers. In Tuscany, we say, "fritta è buona anche una ciabatta" ("even a slipper tastes good if you fry it"). Tuscans love fried food. Frying is our passion and has been for generations.

Without any filling, these flowers are a bit dull for my liking, so I make a stuffing with a mixture of ricotta and acciughe (anchovies). The crisp exterior of the fried flowers combined with the creamy, salty filling creates a real taste sensation.

It isn't easy to find these flowers for sale, but with a bit of luck you might get them from an Italian greengrocer.

Serves 4
Preparation: 30 min
Cooking time: 10 min

INGREDIENTS

8 courgette (zucchini) flowers
160 g (5.5 oz) ricotta
1 sprig mint
Salt
Freshly ground black pepper
8 tinned anchovy fillets,
drained

For the batter:
280 ml (1¼ cup) very cold
sparkling water
200 g (¾ cup) rice flour
Pinch of salt

For frying:
1 litre (4¼ cups) groundnut oil
(alternatively rapeseed oil)

TIP

These taste particularly good
with homemade ricotta
(recipe p. 203).

PREPARATION

Carefully remove the growth at the base of each courgette flower using a knife. Gently remove the stamen, making sure the flower itself remains intact at the top and bottom.

Combine the ricotta and mint leaves, then season with salt and pepper. Insert some of the ricotta mixture into each courgette flower. To make this job easier, the mixture can be transferred into a piping bag first; otherwise, you can just use a simple teaspoon to stuff the flowers. Add an anchovy to each flower, then carefully pinch them closed.

To make the batter, use a balloon whisk to combine the cold sparkling water, rice flour, and salt in a medium bowl. If the mixture is too runny, add a bit more rice flour.

Heat the groundnut oil in a medium pan. As soon as the oil reaches about 180°C/350°F, add the flowers and fry until golden. To ensure you get a nice crust, the temperature of the oil needs to stay at a constant level. At a lower temperature, the flowers will not cook properly all the way through; at a higher temperature, they will burn. If possible, use a kitchen thermometer.

When all the flowers have been fried, serve and eat them quickly before they go cold.

PEPERONATA
STEWED PEPPERS

My sister Ester doesn't really enjoy cooking on a regular basis, but she makes a fantastic version of this simple dish based on a recipe from my father. We always used to eat lots of peperonata, and in giant helpings. Kilos of peppers would be sliced up and cooked with onion. The precise ingredients varied slightly, depending on whatever happened to be available, but vinegar was always included. The end result is a sweet and sour combination that makes an ideal side dish. We love eating this with a chunk of bread. If all goes well, there will be leftovers the next day when it tastes even better.

Serves 4
Preparation: 60 min
Roasting time: 20–25 min
Additional cooking time: 10 min

INGREDIENTS
1 kg (2.2 lbs) bell peppers,
various colours
2 medium white onions
2 garlic cloves
200 ml (1 cup) extra-virgin
olive oil
4 tinned, oil-packed anchovy
fillets, drained
10 pitted black olives
1 tsp tomato concentrate (paste)
2 tbsp white wine vinegar
Salt
10 g (1⅓ tsp) capers
4 parsley stalks

TIP
You can also use long red peppers in this recipe. They are easier to peel and require less cooking time.

PREPARATION
Preheat the oven to 220°C/425°F (fan setting). Line a baking tray with baking paper.

Wash the peppers, then transfer them to the prepared baking tray and roast for about 20–25 minutes, until the skins are nicely browned.

Remove the baking tray from the oven. Transfer the peppers to a large heatproof bowl, place a lid on top, and let them sit for at least 30 minutes (this makes the peppers easier to peel); pull off and discard the skins.

Cut each pepper in half, remove the seeds and membrane, slice into fairly narrow strips, and set aside.

Slice the onions. Peel and dice the garlic.

Heat the oil in a large frying pan. First add the onions, then the garlic. Sauté for a few minutes over a moderate heat until translucent, stirring regularly during this process.

Roughly chop the anchovies and olives, then add them to the pan along with the pepper strips and tomato concentrate. Deglaze the pan with white wine vinegar and season lightly with salt. Simmer for at least 10 minutes over low heat.

Roughly chop the capers, and add them to the pan at the end of the cooking time. Leave to infuse for a couple of seconds, then chop the parsley and stir it in before serving.

TACCOLE AL POMODORO DELLA NONNA TINA
NONNA TINA'S SNOW PEAS IN TOMATO SAUCE

My nonna Tina, my father's mother, usually cooked this dish in spring when snow peas (mangetout) were in season locally. Her recipe makes a hearty and incredibly delicious vegetable side. When I moved from Italy to Berlin, I began reproducing the recipes of my childhood, and this was a dish I cooked regularly. I didn't have much money, so I would buy huge quantities of snow peas and tomatoes and cook enough to last three days. Often I invited friends round, so they also benefited from my desire to recreate the flavours of my homeland. At home, we like to serve these snow peas in tomato sauce alongside a piece of meat. If you can't eat everything, you will be amply rewarded the next day when this dish tastes even better.

Serves 4
Preparation: 20 min
Cooking time: 15–20 min

INGREDIENTS

3 firm, ripe tomatoes
400 g (14 oz) Italian snow peas
(or use runner beans or similar)
1 white onion
1 garlic clove
2 tbsp extra-virgin olive oil
Salt
Freshly ground black pepper

TIP

This dish can be enhanced with a sprinkling of fresh basil leaves. A small, finely chopped chilli in the sauce adds a dash of heat.

PREPARATION

Use a sharp knife to slice a cross into each tomato, then blanch them hot water for about 1 minute. Drain and cool in a bowl of ice water.

Remove the tomatoes from the water and peel off their skins, starting from the crossed incisions you made earlier. Chop the tomatoes into small chunks.

Wash the snow peas under running water, trim the ends, and slice them in half crosswise.

Peel and slice the onion. Peel the garlic clove, then press down firmly with the flat side of a chef's knife to bruise it.

Heat the oil in a large frying pan, add the onion and bruised garlic clove, and sauté over low heat until the onion is soft. Then, add the tomatoes and simmer for a couple of minutes before adding the snow peas.

Add roughly 2 ladles of hot tap water, season with salt and pepper, and cover with a lid. Simmer for about 10 minutes or until the sauce has cooked down to your liking.

CROSTONI SALSICCIA E STRACCHINO
TOAST WITH STRACCHINO CHEESE AND SALSICCIA

When I was a child, we spent eight years in Austria. Over there it was impossible to get genuine Italian salsiccia, a rustic sausage with a particularly spicy and delicious flavour. So every month, when my father travelled to Tarvisio, he would bring back about 50 sausages. My brothers, Giovanni and Simone, would then spend the afternoon baking giant loaves of bread, which they would spread first with stracchino (which is a bit like a cheese spread) and then with salsiccia. Within a couple of days, we would usually have made short work of the 50 sausages and devoured the lot. This crostone has a gratin-style topping that tastes absolutely incredible in combination with the sweet and sour melted cheese. Toasted bread soaks up the flavour of the meat for optimal enjoyment.

Serves 4
Preparation: 10 min
Baking time: 10–15 min

INGREDIENTS
400 g (14 oz) salsiccia
(3–4 fresh sausages)
250 g (9 oz) stracchino
(Italian soft cheese)
1 sprig rosemary
1 sprig thyme
Salt
Freshly ground black pepper
4 large, 1-cm / ½-in-thick slices
white bread

TIP
If you can't find stracchino,
you can use a different
soft cheese.

PREPARATION
Press the sausage meat out of its skin and transfer to a bowl along with the stracchino.

Mash this mixture with a fork until well combined. Strip the rosemary and thyme leaves from the stalks, chop them finely, and add half to the salsiccia and stracchino mixture, stirring everything together. Season with salt and pepper.

Preheat the oven to 200°C/400°F (non-fan setting).

Spread the salsiccia and stracchino mixture evenly over the bread slices using a fork. Transfer the slices of bread onto a lined baking tray, and bake for 10–15 minutes or until golden.

Sprinkle the freshly baked salsiccia crostoni with the rest of the chopped rosemary and thyme and serve warm.

VERDURE FRITTE

FRIED VEGETABLES

My nonna Zita often used to make fried vegetables for meals to mark special occasions—for example, if we had visitors or on public holidays. Different vegetables are sliced into strips, dunked in flour and egg, then fried in hot oil. Fried sage was a particular favourite of mine. In summer, giant sage leaves used to grow around Poggianella, and these were perfect for making crunchy crisps. The verdure go beautifully with fish and meat or can be served as a starter.

Serves 4
Preparation: 30 min
Cooking time: 20 min

INGREDIENTS
Juice of 1 lemon
2 artichokes
3 carrots
2 red onions
4 courgette (zucchini) flowers
Rice flour
10 sage leaves

For the batter:
100 g (½ cup) rice flour
80 ml (5½ tbsp) water

For frying:
2 litres (8½ cups) groundnut oil
Salt

PREPARATION

Mix the lemon juice with cold water in a bowl.

Remove the tough outer green leaves from the artichokes to reveal the pale-yellow leaves around the heart. Peel and trim the stalks. Slice the artichokes in half lengthwise. Use a teaspoon to scrape out the hairs in the centre of the artichokes, then cut the artichokes lengthwise into quarters. Add the prepared artichokes to the lemony water.

Wash and peel the carrots, then slice them lengthwise into long, thin strips. Peel the onion and slice it into thin rings. Gently open the courgette flowers and trim the stalks without cutting them off completely.

Transfer the artichoke quarters to a sieve and drain well. Sprinkle a large cutting board with rice flour and arrange the vegetables on top. Carefully wash the sage leaves and set them aside.

To make the batter: Combine the rice flour and water in a medium bowl. Mix with a balloon whisk until smooth.

Heat the oil in a medium pan to 180°C/350°F (check the temperature using a kitchen thermometer).

Dip each piece of vegetable in the batter, then fry in the hot oil until crisp. Turn each piece several times during the cooking process. Remove the vegetables from the oil and drain on kitchen paper. Continue in the same way until everything has been fried.

Finally, add the washed sage leaves to the batter and fry these, too. Season everything to taste with salt and serve immediately.

VEGETARIANO

VEGETARIAN DISHES

MERCATO DI PRATO

When I was young, we often went to the market in Prato on Mondays with my mother. There, you could get the highest quality products at reasonable prices, and since we always bought in large quantities (we bought produce by the crate), it was worth making the trip.

I still love going there because you can get fresh, seasonal vegetables, usually direct from the farmers. Often, I meet friends "per chiacchierare e mangiare," to chat and to eat some fantastic panino al lampredotto in the market square.

I always feel a deep connection with my native city in this place.

POLENTA GRIGLIATA CON I FUNGHI
GRILLED POLENTA WITH MUSHROOM SAUCE

My mother always cooked lots of polenta to fill us up. If there were any leftovers, she would put the polenta in the fridge to go firm. The next day, she would fry the leftover polenta and serve it with a sumptuous mushroom sauce. She says it reminds her of the mountains that are not far from us. A hearty and delicious recipe for any occasion.

Serves 6
Preparation: 20 min
Cooking time: 20 min

INGREDIENTS
300 g (10 oz) polenta
1 tbsp extra-virgin olive oil
800 g (1.75 lbs) mixed
mushrooms (e.g., chestnut
mushrooms, button mushrooms,
honey mushrooms etc.)
1 bunch parsley
1 garlic clove
30 g (2 tbsp) butter
50 ml (3.5 tbsp) white wine
Salt
Freshly ground black pepper

PREPARATION

Prepare the polenta according to the package instructions, and tip it into a rectangular dish lined with baking paper. Leave to cool completely. (Ideally, make this the previous day and leave it in the fridge overnight.)

Remove the cold polenta from the dish, keeping it in one piece as much as possible, then slice it into bite-size pieces using an oiled knife.

Heat a griddle (ideally made from cast iron) on high and brush it with olive oil, or use a cast iron frying pan instead. As soon as the oil starts to smoke, lay the pieces of polenta on top and fry until they are nicely grilled on both sides.

Clean the mushrooms using a brush, and chop them into small, equal-size pieces.

Wash and chop the parsley; peel the garlic. In a second pan, melt the butter over low heat and sauté the garlic, then add the mushrooms and all but a few tablespoons of the chopped parsley, and increase the heat slightly to cook off some of the moisture. Finally, deglaze the pan with the white wine and season with salt and plenty of ground pepper. Carefully stir mushrooms, making sure they do not fall apart.

Now, cover the pan and cook the mushrooms over a moderate heat for about 15 minutes, stirring occasionally. Transfer the griddled polenta pieces to a serving dish, top with mushrooms, and sprinkle with the reserved chopped parsley to serve.

RISOTTO CON LE BIETOLE

RISOTTO WITH SWISS CHARD

There are lots of different kinds of risotto, but Swiss chard risotto is one of my favourites. I love the vibrant colour the Swiss chard gives this dish. My father is also a big fan of Swiss chard and used to cook it regularly. The important thing is to create a creamy consistency that is almost "soupy." But the rice should still have a bit of bite inside—al dente, as we say in Italy.

Serves 4
Preparation: 30 min
Cooking time: 60 min

INGREDIENTS

For the vegetable stock:
2 carrots
2 celery stalks
1 vine-ripened tomato
1 white onion
1 tsp whole black peppercorns
2 litres (8½ cups) water
Salt

For the risotto:
600 g (1.3 lbs) Swiss chard
Salt
50 g (3½ tbsp) butter
320 g (¾ pound) Carnaroli rice
70 g (2.5 oz) grated Parmesan

Also:
Ice cubes

PREPARATION

To make the vegetable stock, peel and trim the carrots and chop them into fairly big pieces. Remove the leaves from the celery, trim the ends, then split each stalk into 2 or 3 pieces. Halve the tomatoes and the onion.

Heat a dry cast iron skillet on high until it is very hot. Place one half of the onion in the skillet, cut-side down. Let the onion sizzle for about 4 minutes, until it takes on a bit of colour. Remove from the heat. Set the uncooked onion half aside for later.

Next, put the charred onion half, carrots, celery, and tomato in a large saucepan. Add the black peppercorns, cover everything with 2 litres (8 cups) of cold water, and bring to a boil. Then, lower the heat slightly, cover the pan with a lid, and simmer for 30 minutes. Season with salt at the end of the cooking time; strain the stock through a sieve into a large heatproof bowl; discard the vegetables. The vegetable stock is now ready and can be used immediately.

To make the risotto, peel the reserved onion half and chop it finely. Wash the Swiss chard and trim off the ends of the stalks. Separate the leaves from the stalks.

Bring plenty of salted water to a boil in a large pot. Fill a large bowl with ice water.

First, blanch the Swiss chard stalks in the boiling water for approx. 3 minutes, then use tongs to transfer them to the ice water. Next, blanch the leaves for 2 minutes. While the leaves cook, remove the stalks from the ice water and set them aside. When the leaves are finished blanching, use tongs to transfer them to the ice water. Drain and set the leaves aside, keeping them separate from the stalks.

Dab the stalks dry with kitchen paper and chop them into pieces; these will be used as a garnish. Squeeze as much liquid as you can out of the Swiss chard leaves, then place them in a deep container and pour in some of the vegetable stock. Use an immersion blender to purée until smooth. Season with a pinch of salt.

Melt half the butter in a medium pan over moderate heat and sauté the finely chopped onion. Next, stir in the rice. When the rice is almost translucent, start gradually adding vegetable stock, stirring constantly. Halfway through the cooking time for the rice (as indicated on the package), stir in the Swiss chard purée. Continuing cooking the rice, adding a little more stock at a time, until the rice is al dente and the risotto has a soupy consistency. Remove the pan from the heat, stir in the remaining butter and a generous handful of grated Parmesan, and let the risotto rest for 5 minutes with the lid on.

Divide the risotto among plates, garnish with the chopped Swiss chard stalks, and serve.

TORTELLI DI PATATE DI STEFANO
STEFANO'S POTATO-FILLED TORTELLI

My brother Stefano loves filled pasta. He particularly likes making this dish, which he often cooks for special occasions. Tortelli di patate is a typical regional dish in the area around Prato, where I come from. This classic recipe features a simple filling that is easy to whip up. Of course, making the pasta takes a bit of time, but it's also fun, particularly if you get friends and family to join in shaping and cooking the tortelli. This is a dish that benefits from lots of helpers, and it is well worth the effort.

Serves 4 (makes about 20 tortelli)
Preparation: 45 min
Cooking time: 40 min

INGREDIENTS

For the filling:
600 g (1.3 lbs) floury potatoes
60 g (2 oz) grated Parmesan, plus more for serving
50 g (1.75 oz) parsley, finely chopped
1 garlic clove, grated
Freshly grated nutmeg
Salt
Freshly ground black pepper

For the dough:
200 g (1 ⅔ cups) plain (all-purpose) flour
2 eggs
Salt

For the brown butter:
200 g (7 oz) butter
20 sage leaves

PREPARATION

To make the filling, peel and wash the potatoes, cover them with cold water in a large pot, and bring to a boil over a moderate heat. After about 35 minutes, test the potatoes by inserting a fork or toothpick: they should be soft. If not, cook them for a bit longer. Drain the potatoes, then process them through a potato ricer into a large bowl. Add the Parmesan, finely chopped parsley, grated garlic, a pinch of nutmeg, and salt and pepper to taste. Mix well.

While the potatoes are cooking, prepare the pasta dough: Sift the flour into a pile on a work surface, create a well in the top, and crack the eggs into the well. Sprinkle with a pinch of salt, then whisk the eggs with a fork and gradually work in the flour.

Knead the dough until it is smooth and elastic and can be shaped into a ball. Leave it to rest for 30 minutes underneath an upturned bowl. Then, tear off a piece of the dough, covering the remainder so it does not dry out.

Dust the work surface with flour and roughly roll out the dough using a rolling pin. If you have a pasta machine, use it to process the dough until you have a sheet of pasta that is thin, light, and strong. Otherwise, use the rolling pin to roll out the dough until it is nice and thin. Use a cutter to stamp out circles that are roughly 8 cm (3 inches) in diameter.

Place a teaspoon of filling in the centre of each circle. Carefully moisten the edge with water and fold the circle over the filling, pressing the edges together and squeezing out as much air as possible. Completely seal the edges of the pasta parcels by pressing down with the prongs of a fork to make sure the filling does not spill out during cooking.

To make the brown butter, gently heat the butter in a small pan until it begins to foam. Then, carefully continue cooking over moderate heat until small brown crumbs start to rise to the surface. Take care—this happens very quickly, so make sure it doesn't burn! Remove the pan from the heat and filter the brown butter through a fine sieve into a bowl. Add the whole sage leaves and leave to infuse while you cook the pasta.

Cook the pasta parcels in plenty of boiling salted water. When they float to the surface (after about 3–4 minutes), remove them with a slotted spoon, gently shake off any excess water, and transfer them to the bowl with the sage butter; toss gently.

Divide the potato tortelli among plates, sprinkle with Parmesan, and serve.

GNUDI SPINACI E RICOTTA
SPINACH AND RICOTTA DUMPLINGS

Gnudi are delicious little balls made from spinach and ricotta that are cooked, then usually browned in a butter and sage sauce. Gnudi means "naked"—a name they are given because this is essentially just a ravioli filling without the surrounding pasta.

Sabrina, the mother of a close friend of mine, always makes this dish for her five kids. She cooks such superb gnudi that I was absolutely smitten the first time I ate this at her place. Ever since, this has been a regular feature on my own menu, too.

Serves 6
Preparation: 30 min
Cooking time: 35 min

INGREDIENTS
300 g (10.5 oz) spinach
250 g (9 oz) ricotta
1 egg
100 g (3.5 oz) grated Parmesan, plus more for serving
½ tsp freshly grated nutmeg
Salt
Freshly ground black pepper
Plain (all-purpose) flour

For the sauce:
8 sage leaves
150 g (5 oz) butter, cubed
Salt
Freshly ground black pepper

TIP
Caution! Only toss the gnudi very lightly in flour—do not add any additional flour.

PREPARATION
Blanch the spinach in plenty of boiling water until has wilted. Drain immediately and leave to cool, then squeeze out any water—excess water in the spinach can impair the consistency of the gnudi. Chop the spinach with a knife.

In a large bowl, combine the chopped spinach with the ricotta, egg, half the grated Parmesan, and the nutmeg. Season with a pinch each of salt and pepper.

Use your hands to work all the ingredients together until well combined. The result should be a mixture that holds together nicely but is not too firm. Use a table-spoon to take scoops of the mixture and roll these into irregular balls using floured hands. Once you have shaped all the gnudi, toss them in flour and place them on a surface lined with baking paper.

Bring a pot of salted water to a boil, and carefully add the gnudi. As soon as they rise to the surface, scoop them out using a slotted spoon.

Shred the sage leaves and combine them with the cubed butter. Transfer the butter and sage mixture to a large pan, and allow the butter to melt over moderate heat. Gently sauté the cooked gnudi in the sage butter. Avoid stirring (just tilt the pan). Serve warm with Parmesan and freshly ground black pepper.

CRESPELLE ALLA FIORENTINA

SPINACH AND RICOTTA PANCAKES

When my father was still a child, his nonna would make crespelle for him, and you could buy all the ingredients in the bottega, which is like a local corner shop. The range of food on offer there might not be extensive, but the ingredients were always excellent quality. The recipes from this period were simple but nonetheless delicious. In those days, pancakes were made exclusively with egg like an omelette; nowadays, they include flour and milk. This dish is a bit like filled pasta, such as oven-baked cannelloni, with a filling of ricotta and spinach.

Serves 6 (makes fourteen
18-cm / 7-inch pancakes)
Preparation: 60 min
Baking time: 20 min
Resting time: 60 min

INGREDIENTS

For the pancake batter:
3 eggs
250 g (2 cups) plain
(all-purpose) flour
Salt
500 ml (2 cups) whole milk

For the béchamel sauce:
50 g (3½ tbsp) butter
60 g (½ cup) plain
(all-purpose) flour
700 ml (3 cups) whole milk, cold
Salt
Freshly grated nutmeg

For the filling:
450 g (1 lb) spinach, trimmed
and washed
2 tbsp extra-virgin olive oil
1 garlic clove, chopped
400 g (14 oz) ricotta
80 g (3 oz) grated Parmesan
Freshly grated nutmeg
Salt
1 egg

For baking:
125 g (4 oz) Sugo al Pomodoro
(p. 32)
Grated Parmesan
Extra-virgin olive oil

PREPARATION

To make the batter, whisk the eggs with the flour and a pinch of salt. Add the milk in a thin stream, stirring it in with a balloon whisk. Cover the bowl and refrigerate for about 1 hour.

To make the béchamel sauce, melt the butter in a saucepan over a moderate heat. As soon as it has melted, add the flour and stir for a few minutes until golden. Pour in the cold milk in a thin stream, stirring constantly. Let the sauce thicken over moderate heat, then season with a generous pinch of salt and some grated nutmeg.

To make the filling, blanch the spinach in a large pot of boiling water for 1–2 minutes, drain well, squeeze out any liquid, and set aside.

Heat the olive oil and chopped garlic in a pan over low heat. Sweat the garlic, add the spinach, cover with a lid, and continue cooking over low heat for 5 minutes. At the end of the cooking time, remove the lid to allow the remaining liquid to evaporate. Set aside and leave to cool.

Transfer the cooled spinach to a bowl and add the ricotta, 30 g/1 oz grated Parmesan, and a pinch of nutmeg and salt. Roughly combine using a fork, and adjust the seasonings as desired. If the mixture tastes too bland, add some more grated Parmesan. Beat the egg and stir this into the mixture. Set aside.

To cook the pancakes, put a 20-cm (8-inch) nonstick pan over moderate heat. Add a little oil, let it heat up, and pour a thin layer of batter into the pan. Cook for 2–3 minutes or until the edges of the pancake turn golden brown, then flip and continue cooking until done. Transfer to a plate and repeat the process until all the pancakes are cooked.

Preheat the oven to 170°C/325°F (non-fan setting).

Spread each pancake with some of the spinach and ricotta filling, then roll them up. Spread a third of the béchamel sauce across the bottom of an ovenproof dish, place the crespelle on top, and cover with the tomato sauce. Top with the rest of the béchamel, sprinkle with the remaining Parmesan, and drizzle with olive oil. Bake in the centre of the oven for 20 minutes or until golden brown and bubbling at the sides. Eat the crespelle straight from the baking dish while still hot, or, even better, reheat them with a splash of milk the following day.

TOPINI AL POMODORO
MINI GNOCCHI WITH TOMATO SAUCE

In Tuscany, little gnocchi are called topini, meaning "little mice." We didn't often get topini al pomodoro when we were kids, but when we did eat them, I often burned by tongue because I just couldn't wait for them to cool down. This recipe comes from my mother's childhood. She and her siblings were often served this by their domestic help, Anna, who could rustle up topini incredibly quickly. It is a very simple dish with a delicious, fruity flavour. A key component is the classic Sugo al Pomodoro (p. 32).

Serves 4
Preparation: 60 min
Cooking time: 30–40 min

INGREDIENTS

1 kg (2 lbs) floury potatoes (not new potatoes)
300 g (2½ cups) plain (all-purpose) flour
1 egg, whisked
Salt
Semolina, for the work surface
1 litre (4¼ cups) Sugo al Pomodoro (p. 32)

PREPARATION

Put the potatoes in a large saucepan, cover with plenty of cold water, and bring to a boil. From the time when the water comes to a boil, the potatoes will take 30–40 minutes to cook, depending on their size. Test the potatoes by gently inserting a fork. As soon as the centre feels soft, they can be drained. Peel the potatoes while they are still hot.

Sift the flour into a mound on a work surface. Use a potato ricer to process the potatoes directly onto the mound of flour, then add the whisked egg and a pinch of salt.

Knead everything by hand until you have a soft, pliable, but nonetheless firm dough. Cover the dough completely with a tea towel to prevent it from drying out.

Flour your hands, and use your fingertips to roll out the dough on a floured work surface to create 3 sausages, each roughly 1.5 cm (½ inch) in diameter. Use a floured dough scraper or knife to cut each of these into roughly 2-cm/¾-inch-wide pieces. Continue in this way until you have turned all the dough into topini.

As soon as the individual topini have been cut, place them on a chopping board that has been dusted with semolina.

Bring a large pan of salted water to a boil, carefully add the topini, and return the water to a boil. Reduce the heat. Once the topini float to the surface, continue simmering gently for 2 minutes. Remove the topini with a slotted spoon, combine with freshly cooked or reheated tomato sauce, and serve immediately.

PAPPA AL POMODORO
BREAD AND TOMATO SOUP

"Today is a day for pappa al pomodoro," my great-grandmother Zita would say occasionally. She only cooked this bread and tomato soup on certain days, a decision she made entirely at whim, regardless of how hot it was outside or whether she had stale bread leftover for the purpose. My father's grandmother also cooked this on a regular basis. Every Tuscan grandmother has her own recipe because this dish has been part of traditional Tuscan cuisine for generations (since the Middle Ages, to be precise). However, it was originally made without tomatoes.

Just like the Panzanella (p. 84) and Ribollita (p. 94), Pappa al Pomodoro is designed to use leftover bread, and all these dishes benefit from using very dry bread if possible. This dish is extremely popular in Tuscany. In fact, it is so simple and delicious that there is even a song about it: "Viva la pappa col pomodoro"—"Long live pappa al pomodoro"—by Rita Pavone, which is often heard sung loudly while cooking this recipe.

Serves 4
Preparation: 30 min
Cooking time: 30 min

INGREDIENTS
½ leek
3 garlic cloves
1 small fresh red chilli
600 g (1.3 lbs) ripe tomatoes
(or tinned whole peeled
tomatoes, drained)
3 tbsp extra-virgin olive oil,
divided
15 basil leaves
Salt
350 g (12 oz) stale white bread,
thinly sliced
750 ml (3 cups) vegetable stock

TIP
White sourdough bread is an excellent choice for this recipe. If you do not have any stale bread, slice a loaf and dry it out in the oven at a low temperature.

PREPARATION

Trim and carefully wash the leek, peel the garlic, then finely chop both. Slice the chilli (seeds removed) into thin strips.

Remove the core of each tomato using a sharp knife, make a crosswise incision in each, then blanch in hot water for about 1 minute. As soon as the skin begins to come away, remove the tomatoes and transfer to a bowl of ice water. Once the tomatoes have cooled down, carefully remove the skin and slice the tomatoes into quarters.

In a large pan, heat 2 tbsp of olive oil over low heat. Add the garlic, leek, and chilli. Sauté until the leek is translucent.

Wash and shred the basil. Add the tomatoes and basil to the pan with the leek, garlic, and chilli and season with salt. Simmer for 15 minutes over low heat. Add the thinly sliced bread, then gradually pour in the vegetable stock. The amount of stock you will need depends on how old and dry the bread is. The bread should be soaked with the stock.

Simmer the soup, uncovered, over low heat for about 15 minutes or until it has a nice, thick consistency (add more liquid if necessary). Stir occasionally until the pieces of bread have completely disintegrated.

Adjust the seasoning by adding more salt and chilli if required. Remove from the heat and leave the flavours to infuse for 30 minutes before serving.

LA PANZANELLA

TUSCAN BREAD SALAD

Bread plays an important role in Tuscan cuisine. The art of baking has a very long history in this region. Back in the Middle Ages, bread was the staple food among aristocrats and peasants alike. It is a key component in lots of Tuscan dishes.

La panzanella is a classic cucina povera recipe, originally designed to use up leftover bread. Dried bread is soaked in vinegar and water and combined with a few salad ingredients for a delicious meal that is also sustainable. The precise salad ingredients can be varied, but my mother insists that celery, cucumber, basil, and onions are all essential. These ingredients are what create the characteristic taste of this bread salad. You should prepare the salad an hour before eating to allow the flavours to develop. If you don't have any Tuscan bread, choose a light sourdough with a firm crust that won't go too soft. Fresh bread is not suitable; it needs to be at least one day old.

Serves 6
Preparation: 20 min
Soaking time: 45 min

INGREDIENTS

400 g (14 oz) stale Tuscan bread
or other white bread
70 ml (4¾ tbsp) white wine
vinegar
1 red onion
1 cucumber
450 g (1 lb) firm, ripe tomatoes
15 basil leaves

For the dressing:
4 tbsp extra-virgin olive oil
2 tbsp white wine vinegar
Freshly ground black pepper
Salt

TIP

If you only have fresh bread available, slice it into cubes and dry it out in the oven at a low temperature. If you make the panzanella the day before, avoid seasoning it until you are ready to eat, as that impairs the consistency of the salad ingredients.

PREPARATION

Cut the bread into roughly 1-cm/½-inch-thick slices and place these flat in a large ovenproof dish. Pour 250 ml (1 cup) of water over the bread and press down gently with your hands; leave to soften for 40–45 minutes.

Combine the vinegar with 70 ml (¼ cup) of water in a medium bowl. Peel and thinly slice the onion, then transfer it to the bowl with the vinegar mixture. Soak for 15–20 minutes, stirring regularly, then drain well.

Peel the cucumber, slice it in half lengthwise and remove the core with a teaspoon. Slice it very thinly. Core, then slice the tomatoes.

Crumble the soaked bread—if it is too moist, gently squeeze out some of the liquid first— and put the pieces in a large bowl.

Add the soaked onion, sliced tomatoes and cucumber, and torn basil leaves and mix everything together.

Drizzle the panzanella with the olive oil, vinegar, a pinch of pepper, and some salt. Toss well, then transfer to the fridge and leave the flavours to develop for an hour before serving.

INSALATA DI FARRO
SPELT SALAD

Spelt is a very common grain where I come from, and it has been used to make different dishes for many generations. For a long time, it was not cultivated because it was insufficiently lucrative from a commercial perspective. Luckily, spelt's positive nutritional properties have led to its rediscovery, and today it is featured in lots of cold and hot dishes.

Whenever we went on a weekend trip to the seaside, we would take this salad with us for lunch, eating it out of little bowls. It reminds me of hot summer days at the beach, and particularly the sand that would occasionally get blown into our lunch. Not that we cared—we still ate it because it is just so delicious. You can also make this salad with rice rather than spelt, but I prefer the spelt version, since I think it is tastier and more nutritious.

You can vary the salad items if you don't have a particular ingredient; there are endless combinations to suit your personal preference.

Serves 6
Preparation: 20 min
Soaking and cooking time:
depends on the type of spelt

INGREDIENTS
For the spelt:
300 g (10 oz) hulled spelt
1 garlic clove
1 sprig rosemary
3 sprigs thyme
4 tbsp extra-virgin olive oil, plus
more for drizzling
Salt

250 g (9 oz) cherry tomatoes
1 onion
50 g (1.75 oz) semi-mature
Tuscan pecorino
50 g (1.75 oz) pitted black olives
100 g (3.5 oz) cooked peas
50 g (1.75 oz) capers
Basil leaves
Zest of 1 lemon
Juice of ½ lemon

TIP
Instead of spelt, you could use
rice, peeled wheat, or
another grain.

PREPARATION

Soak the spelt according to the package directions. (The soaking and cooking times will depend on the variety.)

After the required soaking time, cook the spelt according to the package directions with the garlic, rosemary, and thyme for about 45 minutes or until al dente. Drain. Remove the herbs and garlic, then transfer the cooked spelt to a large bowl and add the olive oil and a pinch of salt.

Wash and halve the cherry tomatoes. Peel and thinly slice the onions. Dice the Pecorino, roughly chop the olives, and drain the cooked peas and capers. Add everything to the spelt mixture and combine well.

Shred as many basil leaves as you like and add them to the salad, along with the lemon zest and juice. Drizzle with a little oil and stir everything again before serving.

MELANZANE ALLA PARMIGIANA
AUBERGINE PARMIGIANA

My mother says that the first time she came across melanzane alla parmigiana was with Donna Giulia, a friend of her mother's, whose version of this aubergine recipe was so exquisite that it immediately became my mother's favourite dish. She particularly liked making it during our summer holidays in Sicily and Calabria, when aubergines are in season. I also cook parmigiana regularly these days, especially when I'm with my sisters Giuditta and Ester. We have only changed one small detail in terms of the method: instead of frying the sliced aubergines, we bake them in the oven. This makes the parmigiana slightly lighter—and tastier, too, in my opinion. The dish is also less time-consuming to prepare this way.

Serves 6
Preparation: 30 min
Cooking time: at least 60 min
Final oven time: 25–30 min

INGREDIENTS
450 g (1 lb) Sugo al Pomodoro (p. 32)
1 kg (2 lbs) round (or oval) aubergines (eggplant)
100 ml (½ cup) extra-virgin olive oil
200 g (7 oz) smoked provola (alternatively: low-moisture mozzarella)
80 g (3 oz) grated Parmesan
20 basil leaves

TIP
Parmigiana tastes best when eaten lukewarm the day after it is made.

PREPARATION

First, make the sugo al pomodoro (recipe p. 32). The longer the sauce is left to simmer, the more flavour it will have.

Preheat the oven to 180°C/350°F (fan setting) for 20 minutes.

Wash and dry the aubergines, remove the stalks and trim the ends, then cut them lengthwise into 0.5-cm/¼-inch-thick slices. Lay the aubergine slices on two lined baking trays and drizzle with oil. Bake until they are dry and no longer moist (roughly 10 minutes).

Meanwhile, thinly slice the smoked provola and set aside.

To assemble the parmigiana: Spread one-third of the tomato sauce across the bottom of an ovenproof dish. Layer half of the baked aubergine slices on top. Cover with half of the sliced smoked provola, chop and add half of the basil, then 2 tbsp of the Parmesan. Cover with another third of the tomato sauce.

Layer the remaining aubergine slices on top and sprinkle with 2 tbsp of Parmesan. Continue with the rest of the tomato sauce, the rest of the smoked provola, and the remaining basil. Finally, sprinkle with the rest of the Parmesan, making sure everything is well covered. Put the other leaves of the basil on top.

Bake for about 25–30 minutes, until it's bubbly around the edges and browned on top. Remove the parmigiana from the oven. Leave to cool for at least 15 minutes before serving.

FAGIOLI ALL'OLIO

BEANS IN OIL

This classic, cheap, and simple recipe is another great example of cucina povera. In the days before such a wide range of ingredients were available, there was a focus on very simple cooking—usually rice or beans. Meat or fish would only be eaten on the weekend, if you were receiving guests, or maybe for a special celebration that warranted a more elaborate meal. My father often talks about this period. The amazing thing about the regional cuisine in my home area is the way such delicious results are achieved by combining relatively few ingredients in different ways. Good cooking doesn't always have to be particularly sophisticated; what matters is the quality of the individual components. For me, this style of cooking is honest, sincere, and also sustainable—nothing is thrown away. If you have leftovers from this dish, you can turn them into Ribollita (p. 94) or Salsiccia e Fagioli (p. 105).

Serves 4
Preparation: 30 min
Soaking time: depends on type of bean
Cooking time: 60–90 minutes (depending on type of bean)

INGREDIENTS

300 g (10 oz) dried cannellini beans or other dried white beans

For the bouquet garni:
Green outer layer of 1 leek
2 sprigs sage
2 sprigs thyme
1 bay leaf

3 garlic cloves
½ white onion
Salt
Freshly ground black pepper
4 tbsp extra-virgin olive oil, for serving

TIP

The cooking water from the beans can be reused in other recipes. It is packed with starch and flavour and works well, for example, in Salsiccia e Fagioli (p. 105).

PREPARATION

Put the beans in a bowl with plenty of water and soak them according to the package instructions. Drain the beans and rinse them under running water.

To make the bouquet garni, carefully wash the piece of leek green, spread it out, place the herbs on top, and tie everything up using kitchen twine.

Combine the beans, garlic, onion, and bouquet garni in a large pot and cover with 2 litres (8½ cups) of cold water. Bring to a bubble, then reduce the heat to low, cover the pot with a lid, and simmer for about 60–90 minutes, until the beans are cooked. Wait to season with salt until after about 80 minutes; any sooner, and it will cause the beans to develop tough skins. As soon as the beans feel soft, remove the bouquet garni, tip the beans into a sieve, and leave to drain completely. Retain the cooking liquid, as this can be used in other recipes (see tip).

Scoop a ladle of beans onto a serving dish, season with salt and freshly ground black pepper, and drizzle with the olive oil. Serve hot or at room temperature.

LA RIBOLLITA

BEAN STEW

La ribollita is a winter stew and my father's favourite dish—even in summer. Ribollita translates roughly as "reboiled" and is a classic cucina povera recipe for using up old bread combined with seasonal vegetables. This recipe had to be in my cookbook, since it is one of the best-known dishes from my homeland. When my father decides to cook this stew, he loudly announces it the day beforehand because he looks forward to it so much: "Domani c'è la ribollita!" ("Tomorrow we're having ribollita!") When we were little, he always cooked such huge quantities that it would feed all 11 children for several days. He would heat up any leftovers the following day and serve it again and again. This went down well with all of us, because ribollita tastes even better the next day.

Serves 6
Preparation: 30 min
Time to make in advance:
12–24 hrs
Cooking time: 50–140 min
Resting time: 4–8 hrs

INGREDIENTS

350 g (12 oz) cooked cannellini
beans (recipe p. 93; or tinned)

For the stew:
250 g (9 oz) savoy cabbage
300 g (10.5 oz) cavolo nero
(Tuscan kale)
300 g (10.5 oz) Swiss chard
2 large potatoes
1 garlic clove
1 large onion
100 g (3.5 oz) celery stalks
1 large carrot
2 tbsp extra-virgin olive oil
1 (180-g / 6-oz) tin whole peeled
tomatoes
1 litre (4¼ cups) water
2 small pieces Parmesan rind,
trimmed
220 g (½ lb) stale bread
Salt
Freshly ground black pepper

For serving:
Grated Parmesan
Extra-virgin olive oil

PREPARATION

If you're using dried beans, cook them according to the recipe on p. 93. Remove and set aside one-third of the beans, as these will be added at the end. Use a hand blender to purée the remaining beans with about 150 ml (½ cup) of the cooking water until you have a creamy broth (for tinned beans, use all the liquid from the tin in the purée). If the purée seems too thick, add a little more water.

To make the stew, split the savoy cabbage in half, remove the tough inner stalks, wash the leaves, then slice them into julienne strips (thin matchsticks). In the same way, remove the tough inner stalks from the cavolo nero, wash the leaves, and slice them into julienne strips. Wash and roughly chop the Swiss chard.

Peel and dice the potatoes. Finely chop the garlic. Peel and finely chop the onion, celery, and carrot.

Heat the olive oil in a large pot and sauté the chopped onion, celery, and carrot over low heat for about 5 minutes. Add the leafy vegetables, potatoes, tomatoes (breaking them up with a fork first), and the water.

Now, stir in the bean purée, cover with a lid, and bring everything to a boil. When the stew comes to a boil, turn the temperature down to moderate heat, add the Parmesan rinds, cover, and simmer for about 45 minutes, stirring occasionally. The consistency should be runny, so you may need to add more water. Season with salt and pepper, remove the Parmesan rinds, add the whole beans you set aside earlier, and stir everything together. Switch off the hob.

Thickly slice the stale bread, and place about one-third of the slices in the bottom of a soup tureen. Cover with a couple of ladles of the stew, then place another layer of bread on top, cover with stew, and so forth. Continue with these layers until all the ingredients have been used. Refrigerate the ribollita for 4–8 hours before serving.

To serve, heat one portion in a pan, pour it into a bowl, and top with grated Parmesan and a drizzle of olive oil.

CARNE

MEAT

MIA MACELLERIA DI DOMENICO

Whenever I am in my native city of Prato, I visit Domenico in his butcher's shop, Mia Macelleria, on the Piazza Filippo Lippi, right on the little market square. The elongated interior with its high ceilings and rounded brickwork arches has a historic charm. Domenico, who is originally from Sicily, has been working here for 50 years. He has known most of his customers for an eternity, and the same goes for me and my family.

There is a friendly ambience at Domenico's: greetings are exchanged, news is shared, and shopping accomplished. I don't just buy meat in this wonderful shop; I might also pick up a piece of cheese or some antipasti. The products sold here are made by regional farmers and taste fantastic.

When we visit Domenico, we know we are going to get excellent quality and fair prices, and we also regularly benefit from his invaluable advice on how to prepare various ingredients. The recipe for Arista e Patate (p. 129), which is a huge hit with my family, comes from Domenico's never-ending repertoire.

BISTECCA ALLA FIORENTINA
FIORENTINA STEAK

This highly typical Tuscan dish was always regarded as something rather special in my family, since a nice piece of meat comes with a certain price tag, even if it is simple to prepare. In this case, we are dealing with a T-bone steak from the Chianina breed of cattle. This high-quality lean cut is taken from the back of the cow to include both sirloin and tenderloin components. People have been making la bistecca alla Fiorentina for generations; it is the absolute classic of classics, featured on every menu in Tuscany's trattorias. Whether you are eating or cooking bistecca alla Fiorentina, you need to remember the following rules: firstly, the meat needs to be at least 4 fingers thick; secondly, it must be very bloody—in other words, still rare inside; thirdly, it is served and eaten plain, without any sauce; and fourthly, you will ideally need a dining companion, because each piece of meat weighs at least 800 g (1¾ lbs). This is a wonderful, tender, aromatic, and succulent cut of meat.

In my family, this was only served on special occasions, particularly if we wanted to offer a fine meal to guests with the hope of making a "bella figura" in the process. To be honest, there was always good food at our house, but some dishes were saved for when we had visitors. You could say I've carried on that tradition; cooking for other people is the greatest pleasure for me, and it is such a joy to serve the very finest food on these occasions. La bistecca alla Fiorentina is definitely one of those dishes.

Serves 4
Resting time: 120 minutes
Cooking time: 10–12 mi

INGREDIENTS

1 T-bone steak (approx. 1 kg / 2 lbs,
at least 4 cm / 1.5 inch thick)
Maldon salt
Freshly ground black pepper
Extra-virgin olive oil

TIP

Bistecca alla Fiorentina should always be cooked on a charcoal grill because the coals give the meat a superb flavour. Cannellini beans (p. 93) go beautifully with Fiorentina steak.

PREPARATION

Remove the T-bone steak from the fridge 120 minutes before cooking, and dab it dry with kitchen paper. (The meat must be brought fully to room temperature before it is put on the grill.) Place the steak on a plate lined with kitchen paper.

Set up a charcoal grill for high heat. As soon as ashes appear on top of the charcoal, place the meat on the metal rack.

The grilling time depends on the thickness and weight of the steak, as well as how you like your meat cooked. A very bloody steak requires an internal temperature of 48°C/118°F; a medium-rare steak requires 52–55°C/125–131°F. In general, you should not exceed a temperature of 60–65°C/140–149°F. The temperature can be checked with the help of a meat thermometer, but with time you will be able to achieve the same results based on experience.

Depending on how thick the meat is, cook the first side for 3–5 minutes without moving it. Then, flip the steak and continue cooking for 3–5 minutes. Important: never pierce the meat! You don't want the juices to escape. If the meat is very thick, turn the T-bone steak so it sits directly on the grill with the bone facing down, and cook for about 1–2 minutes in this vertical position.

After cooking, transfer the steak to a chopping board, cover with foil, and let it rest for about 10 minutes to allow the juices to be evenly reabsorbed.

Finally, season with Maldon salt and freshly ground pepper, and drizzle with a few drops of olive oil.

POLPETTE AL POMODORO

MEATBALLS IN TOMATO SAUCE

Polpette al Pomodoro is an Italian recipe for using up minced meat. Leftover meatballs are reheated in tomato sauce the next day to make them soft again. Tomato sauce is always a great way to make food really delicious if it is being reheated.

Serves 6 (makes approx.
26 meatballs)
Preparation: 20 min
Cooking time: 30 min

INGREDIENTS

30 g (1 oz) stale white bread
400 g (14 oz) beef and pork
mince (ground meat)
1 pinch dried oregano
1 pinch freshly grated nutmeg
1 tbsp parsley leaves, chopped
28 g (1 oz) grated Parmesan
1 egg
Fine salt
Freshly ground black pepper
4 tbsp extra-virgin olive oil
300 g (10 oz) Sugo al
Pomodoro (p. 32)
Basil leaves

PREPARATION

First, chop the bread into small chunks, put it in a food processor, and blitz until you have fine breadcrumbs. If you don't have any stale bread, you can use 30 g/4 tbsp shop-bought breadcrumbs instead.

Put the beef and pork mince in a large bowl. Add the oregano, grated nutmeg, chopped parsley, grated parmesan, and the prepared breadcrumbs. Next, add the egg and use your hands to work all the ingredients together. Season with salt and pepper and continue manually working the ingredients until you have a smooth mixture.

Use a spoon to scoop out portions of the meat mixture, each weighing roughly 20 g (0.7 oz), then roll them into balls between the palms of your hands. You should get about 26 meatballs in total.

As soon as the meatballs are formed, heat the oil in a nonstick pan and fry the meatballs on each side for a couple of minutes, until browned.

Season the tomato sauce with salt and pepper, add the fried meatballs, and cook over low heat for 15–20 minutes, until the meatballs are cooked through. Sprinkle with basil leaves and serve.

SALSICCIA E FAGIOLI

SAUSAGE AND BEANS

Beans are a very typical ingredient in my region and are used in lots of traditional dishes. They were introduced here after being discovered in America (along with potatoes and tomatoes), and nowadays they are an important part of Tuscan food culture. The bakeries where I come from cook bread in wood-fired ovens, and it is very common to cook some beans in a terracotta pot alongside the final batch of loaves. The beans are then sold in the morning and used, for example for making this recipe.

Salsiccia e fagioli is an everyday recipe because it doesn't take long to make, and the ingredients are not expensive. Since this is a fairly rich dish, I like to cook it on cold winter days. I soak the fagioli in water with a bit of rosemary, then simmer them over low heat the following day. This ensures that the beans have the best flavour and consistency. Fagioli cooked this way are a guaranteed crowd-pleaser.

Serves 6
Preparation: 20 min
Cooking time: 40 min

INGREDIENTS

600 g (1.3 lbs) cooked cannellini beans (recipe p. 93) or tinned
1 tbsp extra-virgin olive oil
1 garlic clove
6 sage leaves
6 fresh salsiccia (Italian sausages), approx. 100 g / 3.5 oz each, casings removed
50 ml (3.5 tbsp) red wine
1 tbsp tomato concentrate (paste)
100 ml (½ cup) passata (tomato purée)
Salt
Freshly ground black pepper
1 sprig rosemary
Toasted Tuscan or sourdough bread, for serving

TIP

The beans should be soft but not falling apart.

PREPARATION

If using dried beans, cook them according to the recipe on p. 93, then drain them and reserve the liquid in a separate bowl. If using tinned beans, drain them and reserve the liquid.

In a wide frying pan, heat the olive oil and sauté the crushed garlic clove and sage leaves for a couple of minutes. Add the skinned salsiccia and fry for 3–4 minutes, stirring occasionally. Deglaze the pan with the wine and ensure that the alcohol has completely evaporated.

Mix the tomato concentrate with 200 ml (1 cup) hot water in a small bowl, then add the mixture to the pan, along with the passata. Season with salt and pepper and cook over low heat, uncovered, for 35–40 minutes.

Add the beans to the pan with the salsiccia. Simmer to allow the flavours to blend. Season with salt and pepper. The consistency should be thick and soupy; you may need to add some of the reserved water from the beans to achieve the desired result. If the sauce is too runny, continue simmering over low heat.

Add the chopped rosemary, drizzle with olive oil, and serve with toasted Tuscan or sourdough bread.

TAGLIATA DI MANZO CON GRANA E RUCOLA

RIB-EYE STEAK WITH ROCKET AND PARMESAN

The thing I love about this dish is that it is so light and delicious. If you find Bistecca alla Fiorentina (p. 101) a bit too much, this is a great alternative. It is similar to what the French call entrecôte (sirloin steak). The beef is served on a rocket salad topped with slices of Parmesan.

Serves 4
Resting time: 60–120 minutes
Cooking time: 15 min

INGREDIENTS

800 g (1.75 lbs) rib-eye steak,
4–5 cm (1½–2 inches) thick
80 g (3 oz) rocket (arugula)
100-g / 3.5-oz piece of Parmesan,
thinly sliced
Extra-virgin olive oil
Flaked sea salt
Freshly ground black pepper

TIP

I recommend sprinkling the meat with coarse salt 2–4 hours beforehand, then refrigerating it, even if this is not standard practice in Tuscany. This approach gives it a more well-rounded flavour.

PREPARATION

Remove the rib-eye steak from the fridge at least 1 hour ahead of time; it will not cook properly from cold. Wash and dry the rocket. Thinly slice the Parmesan and set aside.

Set up a charcoal grill for high heat. As soon as ashes appear on top of the charcoal, place the meat on the metal rack. Grill for about 3 minutes on one side. Flip the meat with tongs (avoid using a fork, as you do not want to pierce the surface of the meat and cause the juices to run out) and continue cooking for 3–4 minutes. To make sure the meat is cooked medium rare, you can use a meat thermometer. The core temperature should be about 52–54°C/125–129°F.

Remove the meat from the grill to a chopping board, cover with foil, and let it rest for 5 minutes to allow the juices to be evenly reabsorbed. Then, slice the steak into several strips using a sharp knife. Arrange a bed of rocket on a serving plate and top with the meat, followed by the sliced Parmesan. Add a dash of olive oil, some salt flakes (or coarse salt), and freshly ground pepper to serve.

FARAONA IN UMIDO
BRAISED GUINEA FOWL

My father was born in the Marche region, where Faraona is a typical dish. Faraona alla cacciatora (guinea fowl cooked hunter-style) is a classic family recipe that he inherited. He cooks it for us on special occasions, such as at Christmas. The meat from a guinea fowl is slightly firmer than the more familiar chicken. It is exceptionally tasty, and when braised in tomato sauce with olives, the meat becomes tender and acquires a fruity, aromatic flavour that is irresistible.

You can also use this technique to cook other kinds of meat, such as rabbit, venison, or wild boar.

Serves 6
Preparation: 20 min
Cooking time: 60 min

INGREDIENTS

1 (1.2 kg/2.5-pound) guinea fowl,
prepared and quartered
Salt
Freshly ground black pepper
1 shallot
3 garlic cloves
Leaves from 2 sprigs rosemary
4 tbsp extra-virgin olive oil
100 ml (½ cup) dry white wine
200 ml (¾ cup) chicken stock
2 tbsp tomato concentrate
(paste)
100 g (3.5 oz) pitted black olives
(for example Taggiasca)
Sliced bread, for serving

PREPARATION

Season each piece of guinea foul with salt and pepper.

Peel and finely chop the shallot, peel and crush the garlic cloves, and finely chop the rosemary. Heat the olive oil in a cast iron pan over moderate heat. Place the guinea fowl pieces in the hot pan, skin-side down, and cook until they are evenly browned. Deglaze the pan with the white wine, ensuring that the alcohol has cooked off. Add the shallot, garlic, and rosemary and sauté gently over moderate heat for about 20 minutes.

Heat the chicken stock in a small saucepan. Stir in the tomato concentrate, then pour 60 ml/¼ cup of the tomato broth mixture over the guinea fowl. Continue cooking for 30 minutes. After 10 minutes, add the olives. During this cooking process, gradually add the rest of the stock–tomato concentrate mixture to ensure that the sauce does not become too thick. By adding stock at small intervals, the meat will cook better and become soft and succulent.

Serve with sliced bread. As you eat, dip chunks of bread in the wonderful guinea fowl–infused sauce. At this point, Italians like to say, "fare la scarpetta" ("make the little shoe"), in reference to the shape of the bread used to mop up the sauce.

TRIPPA ALLA FIORENTINA
FLORENTINE-STYLE TRIPE

Trippa alla Fiorentina is a traditional Tuscan dish. The tripe is cooked for a long time in a tomato sauce to create a fabulous meal. Some people are not keen on tripe, but when they give this recipe a go they are generally pleasantly surprised by the special flavour. My mother's mother, Nonna Marisa, often cooked Trippa alla Fiorentina because my grandfather loved this dish so much. This recipe is the standard Tuscan version.

Serves 4
Preparation: 30 min
Cooking time: 90-120 min

INGREDIENTS
1 kg (2 lbs) cooked tripe
1 carrot
1 celery stalk
1 white onion
1 salsiccia (Italian sausage),
approx. 100 g / 3.5 oz)
4 tbsp extra-virgin olive oil
1 garlic clove
3 bay leaves
50 ml (3.5 tbsp) white wine
300 g (10 oz) tinned whole
peeled tomatoes
Salt
Freshly ground black pepper
Dried red chilli flakes
1 (5×3 cm / 2×1-inch) piece
Parmesan rind
200 ml (1 cup) vegetable stock
(p. 66)
100 g (3.5 oz) grated Parmesan
30 g (2 tbsp) butter
Chopped parsley leaves
Bread, for serving

PREPARATION
To make Florentine-style tripe, the first thing you need to do is visit your trusted butcher to buy tripe that have already been cleaned and cooked. Thinly slice the tripe, then wash the pieces under running water and drain them thoroughly.

Peel and finely dice the carrot. Wash, halve, and finely dice the celery. Peel, halve, and dice the onion. Remove the casing from the salsiccia and pinch it into small pieces.

Heat the olive oil in a large pan, and gently fry the salsiccia. Crush the garlic clove, add it to the pan, along with the chopped vegetables and bay leaves, and sweat the vegetables for 5 minutes over low heat. Add the tripe and sauté, stirring occasionally with a wooden spoon. Deglaze the pan with the white wine and allow it to evaporate completely. Now, break up the peeled tomatoes, add them to the pan, and season with salt and pepper and the chilli flakes.

Use a sharp knife to make incisions in the surface of the Parmesan rind (this allows the rind to give the dish even more flavour), brush off the rind thoroughly, and add it to the pan. Cover the pan with a lid and continue cooking the tripe over low heat for 90–120 minutes, pouring in a little of the hot stock at a time and turning the tripe pieces regularly until they are neither too soft, nor too rubbery. If the texture is still rubbery, you should cook the tripe a bit longer.

At the end of the cooking time, add the grated Parmesan and butter, then leave the pan to stand for 5 minutes. Sprinkle the Florentine-style tripe with chopped parsley, and serve hot with some bread.

PORCHETTA
ITALIAN ROAST PORK

My family was introduced to this recipe by my brother-in-law Lorenzo after he married my sister Maria Rachele. He had a wood-fired oven at home, which is what we, along with my brother Giacomo, used to cook this roast. The recipe originally comes from Umbria, where they also cook porchetta in a wood oven and then sell it as a kind of street food. The crucial thing here is to get the right balance between the spices. The following recipe is for a particularly tender and aromatic roast—I decided long ago that this was a perfect dish for a celebratory dinner.

Serves 20
Preparation: 50 min
Cooking time: 5 hrs

INGREDIENTS
1 (5-kg / 11-pound) slab of pork belly, including rind
1 (1.2-kg / 2½-pound) pork loin
1 kg (2 lbs) pork liver

For the spice mix:
40 g (1.5 oz) fresh wild fennel, roughly chopped
10 g (0.4 oz) fennel seeds
6 garlic cloves, chopped
10 g (0.4 oz) fresh sage, chopped
30 g (1 oz) fresh rosemary, chopped
80 g (3 oz) fine salt (2% of the total weight of the meat)
15 g (0.5 oz) ground pepper

For cooking:
5 tbsp extra-virgin olive oil
Coarse salt
500 ml (2 cups) white wine
500 ml (2 cups) water

TIP
Slices of porchetta make excellent finger food served in panini.

PREPARATION

First, check that any excess fat has been removed from the pork belly and ensure the pork rind (skin) is clean (I recommend asking your butcher to do this for you). The pork belly has the shape of a flattened rectangle. Make incisions in the rind, which will help you season and tie it up later, then place the pork belly rind-down on a clean work surface with one long side of the rectangle facing you.

Starting at the right end of the rectangle, use a long, sharp knife to cut horizontally above the rind, working your way toward the centre, yet stopping when you get about one-third of the way through the pork belly. Next, slice horizontally from the left side toward the centre separating the meat from the rind and leaving a roughly 5-cm (2-inch) section of the rind attached to meat. If the meat is thicker on one end slice horizontally through that section, leaving a few centimetres at the end, and fold it out to create a more even layer. Brush liberally with olive oil.

Combine the wild fennel with the fennel seeds, garlic, sage, rosemary, salt, and pepper and rub this in so the meat is entirely covered. Make sure you reach every area that has been cut. The spices should stick to the meat. Lay the pork loin and liver in the centre of the prepared pork belly, fold the flaps of pork belly meat up and around the pork loin and liver, and wrap everything in the rind. Tie the whole thing closed with butcher's twine, then use a sharp knife to make small holes in the skin every 2–3 cm (1 inch) to allow you to insert a needle and butcher's twine. Use a long needle to sew up the porchetta until it is completely bound together. Remove the butcher's twine. Use the tip of a knife to make multiple incisions in the skin. Rub some olive oil into the surface, sprinkle with coarse salt, and wrap in aluminium foil.

Preheat the oven to 200°C / 400°F / (non-fan setting). Place the porchetta on the central shelf and slide a baking tray underneath to catch the juices that will escape during cooking. Roast for 2½ hours. Check the amount of liquid in the baking tray every 20 minutes, and gradually add the wine and water, alternately.

After 2½ hours, remove the foil and continue cooking for another 2½ hours at 220°C / 425°F (fan setting). Continue adding liquid to the baking tray during this time. Gradually, a crisp crust will develop on the porchetta. Make sure the surface does not burn; if necessary, cover with foil again. At the end of the cooking time, the porchetta should have reached a temperature of 82°C / 180°F (check this using a meat thermometer). If you do not have a thermometer, the following rule of thumb applies: 1 hour cooking time per 1 kg (2 lbs) meat. After cooking, wait at least 3 hours before carving the porchetta. Serve the meat in 1-cm-/½-inch-thick slices.

RISO IN BRODO DI SILVIA E ROBERTO

SILVIA AND ROBERTO'S RICE IN CHICKEN STOCK

This simple but delicious recipe is fresh, tasty, and nourishing. In my family, we traditionally make this at Easter.

Everyone is given their own egg to be cracked open and placed in the rice. In my mother's family, they add grated lemon zest, and now my father's family does, too. An important detail here is the hearty homemade chicken stock. I also like to cook this recipe if someone has a cold, whether it's summer or winter.

Serves 4
Preparation: 15 min
Cooking time: 3–4 hrs

INGREDIENTS

For the chicken stock:
2 carrots
2 celery stalks
1 white onion
1 sprig parsley
4 sprigs thyme
2 bay leaves
10 whole black peppercorns
1 tbsp salt
1 (2-kg / 4.5-lb) stewing hen, jointed

4 eggs, at room temperature
Salt
Freshly ground black pepper
280 g (10 oz) Roma rice
30 g (1 oz) grated Parmesan
Zest of 1 lemon

TIP

The excess stock can be used for all sorts of other recipes and keeps in the fridge for 4–5 days.

PREPARATION

To make the stock: Wash, then roughly chop the carrots and celery. Halve and peel the onion. Place both onion halves, cut-side down, in a hot, dry pan over high heat until pale brown. Tie the parsley, thyme, and bay leaf together to make a bouquet garni, and put it in a large pot with the onion halves, carrots and celery, peppercorns, salt, the chicken pieces, and 5 litres (1⅓ gallon) of cold water.

Slowly bring to a boil, then lower the heat and simmer gently just above boiling point for 3–4 hours with the lid half covering the pan. Every so often, scoop off any cloudy material from the surface. At the end of the cooking time, remove the chicken, onions, vegetables, and herbs with a slotted spoon. The chicken can then be used in a different dish (for example, added to a salad or omelette). Strain the broth through a sieve lined with a cloth.

Place the room temperature eggs in a saucepan of boiling water and cook for 8 minutes—the yolks will still be soft. At the end of the cooking time, immerse the eggs in cold water. Peel and quarter the eggs.

Bring 2 litres (8½ cups) of the broth back to a boil in a medium pan and season with salt and pepper. Add the rice and cook until al dente, then turn off the heat.

Serve in soup dishes with the eggs on top and a sprinkling of Parmesan and lemon zest.

POLLO FRITTO DEL BABBO ROBERTO

PAPA ROBERTO'S FRIED CHICKEN

My father says that, for him, food is mainly about memories: "un tuffo nel passato," (a leap into the past). Memories of his childhood, of times gone by, and of people from that period. For him, that is the greatest motivation to cook.

One very important recipe for him is his mother's pollo fritto. My nonna Tina used to make this for special occasions, such as at Christmas or on Sundays. He still remembers today how crisp it was on the outside, without losing any of its firm texture or becoming too dry. Nonna Tina never wrote down her recipe for pollo fritto, so my father had to try out all sorts of approaches to achieve his mother's perfect result. Today he is our expert, and he takes responsibility for this dish in our family. It is so delicious that my brother Giacomo still regularly asks: "Babbo fai il pollo fritto?" (Dad, are you making fried chicken?).

Serves 6
Preparation: 20 min
Time to make in
advance: 90 min
Cooking time: 40 min

INGREDIENTS
1 corn-fed chicken

For the marinade:
1 garlic clove
1 sprig rosemary
1 sprig sage
1 sprig marjoram
Zest and juice of 2 lemons
3 tbsp extra-virgin olive oil
Salt
Freshly ground black pepper

For the breadcrumb coating:
300 g (2½ cups) plain
(all-purpose) flour
300 g (10.5 oz) breadcrumbs
3 eggs
Salt

For frying:
3 litres (12 cups) groundnut or
sunflower oil

To serve:
Lemon wedges

PREPARATION

Cut the chicken in half vertically, separate the legs and wings, then cut it into bite-size pieces and set aside.

Finely chop the garlic, rosemary, sage, and marjoram, and transfer to an ovenproof dish. Add the grated lemon zest, lemon juice, and 1–2 tbsp olive oil, and season with salt and pepper. Mix well, then coat the chicken pieces in the marinade. Cover and leave in the fridge for 1 hour.

Put the flour and breadcrumbs in separate deep plates or wide bowls. In a third plate or bowl, whisk the eggs with a pinch of salt. Coat the pieces of chicken on both sides with flour, then dip into the beaten egg. All the pieces of meat need to be well coated with egg. Finally, toss the pieces of meat in the breadcrumbs. Place the coated chicken on a lined baking tray, cover, and leave in the fridge for 30 minutes.

Heat the groundnut oil to 180°C/350°F in a deep pan. Don't skimp on the oil; the chunks of meat should be roughly half covered. Fry just a handful of pieces at once, as you don't want to overcrowd the pan. After about 5 minutes, turn the pieces and continue cooking for at least 5 minutes, until the chicken has turned a nice golden colour. You will need to make sure you use a slotted spoon to remove any of the breadcrumb coating that has sunk to the bottom of the pan; otherwise, it will burn.

Scoop out the fried chicken pieces with the slotted spoon and transfer them to a plate or tray lined with kitchen paper. Serve hot or keep warm in the oven until you are ready to eat. Serve the pollo fritto with lemon wedges, which you can squeeze over the meat.

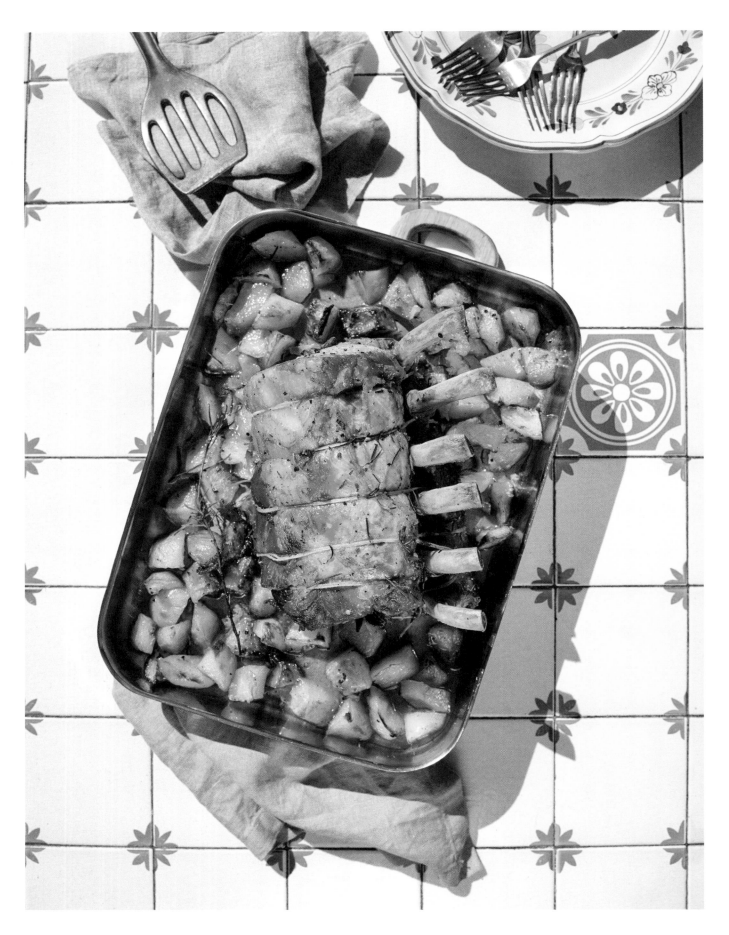

ARISTA E PATATE
ROAST POTATOES AND PORK

There are lots of birthdays in my family. Sometimes it feels like they are almost every day because there are lots of us and we always celebrate together. On these occasions, my mother makes delicious Arista e Patate, crispy roast pork with potatoes.

This recipe comes with a story: When my parents returned home after spending several years in Austria, my mother had the idea of opening a restaurant, and she wanted it to be at our house, La Poggianella. She visited our friendly butcher, Domenico (p. 98), and asked him for suitable recipes, which she then tried out on friends. Mum's idea did not come to fruition, but the following recipe—as suggested by our Domenico—became part of our family tradition.

Serves 6
Preparation: 20 min
Time to make in
advance: 120 min
Cooking time: 50–60 min

INGREDIENTS

Leaves from 2 sprigs rosemary
Leaves from 2 sprigs thyme
6 sage leaves
1.3 kg (3 lbs) pork loin,
at room temperature
2 garlic cloves, chopped
Salt
Freshly ground black pepper
450 g (1 lb) waxy potatoes
200 ml (¾ cup) white wine

TIP

Make sure you put the potatoes underneath the roasting meat, so they cook in the roasting juices. This adds a distinctive flavour to the dish.

PREPARATION

Roughly chop the herbs and divide them in half. Using a sharp knife, carefully separate the layer of fat on the pork loin from the meat, but not so it comes away completely. The aim is to make a kind of pocket. Stuff the garlic and half of the chopped herbs into this pocket, and season everything with salt and pepper.

Close the pocket by bringing the flaps of meat back together, and tie up the roast. First, wrap some kitchen twine crosswise around the lower section of the roast, tie a knot, then wrap it lengthwise around the meat, tying the ends together. Now, wrap the twine lengthwise around the other long side and fasten with a knot. Wrap the twine several times crosswise around the roast along the ribs, and fasten with a knot. This technique ensures that the layer of fat remains firmly attached to the meat.

Preheat the oven to 180°C/350°F (non-fan setting). Carefully wash and dry the potatoes, peel and chop them into large, equal-size cubes, and set aside.

Brown the meat in a cast iron pan on all sides, without piercing the surface—this is to ensure the pores in the meat are sealed and the juices are retained. When the meat has browned nicely, pour in the white wine. Wait a few moments, then use tongs to place the meat directly on the top oven rack; place a baking tray on the rack below the roast to catch the juices. Preserve the liquid from searing the meat in the pan. The cooking time depends on the size of the meat and will be roughly 50–60 minutes. The meat is done when it reaches a core temperature of 62–65°C/143–149°F.

In the final 30 minutes, transfer the potatoes to the baking tray under the roast and sprinkle them lightly with salt. You don't need to add any oil, as the fat surrounding the pork melts as it cooks. Roast the potatoes under the meat for about 30 minutes. If the meat is done earlier, the potatoes can continue to cook separately.

Remove the roast from the oven, place the meat on a chopping board, and leave it to rest for 10 minutes. Meanwhile, over low heat, gently simmer down the cooking juices saved from browning the meat earlier. Completely remove the kitchen twine from the meat.

To serve, carve slices of the roast, arrange them on a platter with the potatoes, sprinkle with the remaining herbs, and pour the cooking juices over everything.

RAGÙ TOSCANO

TUSCAN RAGOUT

Ragù Toscano is a tomato and minced meat sauce. Unlike the standard Italian minced meat sauce, ragù alla Bolognese, this sauce is made with salsiccia and aromatic herbs, such as rosemary, sage, and bay leaf, not to mention plenty of tomatoes. The result is a very special sauce that is packed with flavour. If you want, you can add even more interest with some chicken liver or heart, but that is not essential. The sauce can be eaten with your favourite pasta or some polenta. It is also the basis for the Sedani alla Pratese recipe (p. 133). This sauce can be frozen or will keep in the fridge for up to 3 days.

Serves 6

Preparation: 20 min

Cooking time: 120 min

INGREDIENTS

3 sage leaves

1 sprig rosemary

1 bay leaf

1 red onion

2 celery stalks

1 carrot

1 garlic clove

4 tbsp extra-virgin olive oil

450 g (1 lb) salsiccia (Italian sausages)

1 kg (2 lbs) minced beef (ground beef)

150 ml (¾ cup) red wine

Salt

Freshly ground black pepper

Pinch of freshly grated nutmeg

1 tbsp tomato concentrate (paste)

800 g (1.75 lbs) tinned whole peeled tomatoes

PREPARATION

Use some kitchen twine to tie the sage leaves, rosemary, and bay leaf together for a bouquet garni.

Finely chop the onion, celery, carrot, and garlic clove. Heat the oil in a large pan, and sauté everything over moderate heat for 10 minutes, stirring constantly, until the vegetables are soft.

Remove the casings from the salsiccia, pinch it into little pieces, then add to the pan and fry. As soon as the sausage starts to exude fat, add the minced meat and bouquet garni. Cook everything over moderate heat until the meat is well cooked.

Deglaze the pan with the red wine, continuing to cook until the liquid has evaporated. Season with salt, pepper, and the grated nutmeg.

Dissolve the tomato concentrate in 250 ml/1 cup hot water and add it to the pan, stirring well to combine.

Break up the peeled tomatoes and add them to the pan so the minced meat is covered. The consistency of the sauce should be fairly thick; add hot water if required.

Bring the meaty sauce to a boil, then cook, uncovered, over very low heat for about 2 hours, stirring occasionally and adding hot water if required. At the end of the cooking time, remove the bouquet garni. The desired result is a soft and creamy sauce.

SEDANI ALLA PRATESE DELLA NONNA TINA

NONNA TINA'S STUFFED CELERY

Stuffed celery is a Sunday recipe and a special dish from my home city. It is almost only ever eaten in Prato, and it tastes incredible because the celery and meat sauce complement each other so beautifully. This dish requires a bit of patience to prepare, but it is well worth it.

My father, Roberto, says he only successfully replicated his mother's sedani alla Pratese on one occasion, then never again. My brother Tommaso also cooks superb sedani alla Pratese. He works as a chef in one of Prato's most traditional restaurants, where this dish is always on offer. He has taught me how it is made. The foundation for this recipe is the Ragù Toscano (p. 130).

Serves 6
Preparation: 30 min
Cooking time: 190 min

INGREDIENTS
1 recipe Ragù Toscano (p. 130)
4 heads celery

For the filling:
300 g (10 oz) veal mince
(ground veal)
150 g (5 oz) finely
chopped mortadella
50 g (1.75 oz) grated Parmesan
½ garlic clove
2 eggs
Salt
Freshly ground black pepper
Freshly grated nutmeg

For the batter:
1 egg
100 g (¾ cup) plain
(all-purpose) flour
100 ml (⅓ cup) cold whole milk
Salt

For frying:
1 litre (4¼ cups) groundnut
or sunflower oil

50 g (1.75 oz) grated Parmesan

PREPARATION

Prepare the Ragù Toscano according to the recipe (p. 130).

Carefully wash the celery, remove any stringy sections from the thicker stalks, and slice it into roughly 8-cm/3-inch-long pieces. Blanch the celery pieces in boiling salted water for 4–5 minutes and drain in a sieve. Leave to drain and cool thoroughly.

To make the filling, combine the veal mince, chopped mortadella, grated Parmesan, garlic, and eggs, and season with salt, pepper, and some nutmeg.

Fill half of the celery stalks with this mixture, pressing down well to ensure that it all sticks together, then put the other stalks on top like a lid, pressing down carefully.

To make the batter, beat the egg in a bowl with a balloon whisk. While continuing to whisk constantly, alternately add the flour and the very cold milk. Season with salt. The batter should be thick; if it is too runny, add a bit more flour.

Heat the oil to 180°C/350°F in a deep pan. Dip the filled celery stalks in the batter, then fry them until golden. After frying, remove the celery with a slotted spoon and drain on a baking tray lined with kitchen paper to remove the excess oil.

Preheat the oven to 180°C/350°F (non-fan setting).

Spread a layer of ragù Toscano in the bottom of a baking dish, place a layer of fried sedani on top (one alongside the other), and cover with more ragù. Continue this process until all the celery stalk parcels have been added. Cover with the remaining grated Parmesan and bake for 20 minutes.

BRACIOLINE ALLA LIVORNESE
VEAL SCHNITZEL IN TOMATO SAUCE

When my father was little, his mother, Tina, would often fry him a very thin veal schnitzel on a Friday. The following day, she would use the rest of the meat to make Bracioline alla Livornese. This dish is named after Livorno, a seaside city in Tuscany. Nonna Tina tossed the meat in flour, egg, and breadcrumbs before frying it—and my father used to help her. Preparing the meat alla Livornese was a bit more time-consuming than the previous day's recipe, since the schnitzel was added to a rich tomato sauce. My father still enthuses about it today.

Serves 4
Preparation: 15 min
Cooking time: 70 min

INGREDIENTS
For the sauce:
1 garlic clove
Pinch of dried chilli flakes
2 tbsp extra-virgin olive oil
300 g (1¼ cups) passata
(tomato purée)
4 sage leaves
Salt
Freshly ground black pepper

For the breadcrumb coating:
200 g (1⅔ cups) plain
(all-purpose) flour
200 g (7 oz) breadcrumbs
4 eggs

4 thin veal cutlets (approx.
300 g/10 oz total)

For frying:
300 ml (1 cup) groundnut
or sunflower oil

TIP
This recipe is ideal for using up leftover meat the next day. Of course, you can also serve the schnitzel without tomato sauce to save time.

PREPARATION
Peel and finely chop the garlic; dice the chilli.

Heat the olive oil in a wide pot or high-sided saucepan and sweat the garlic, sage, and chilli. As soon as the garlic is acquiring some colour, add the passata, cook for about 10 minutes, then season with salt and pepper. Set the pot aside.

Put the flour and breadcrumbs in separate wide bowls or deep plates. Beat the eggs in a third bowl or plate.

Use a meat mallet to bash the veal cutlets until very thin, then dust them lightly with flour on both sides. Dip each schnitzel into the beaten egg until well covered. Allow the excess egg to drip off, then toss each schnitzel in the breadcrumbs, pressing the coating repeatedly with your hands to make sure it sticks. If you want a thicker breadcrumb coating, repeat this process.

Heat the groundnut oil in a high-sided frying pan. Add the coated meat and fry. Since the meat is very thin, it will not take long to cook. As soon as the schnitzels are golden brown, remove them from the pan, allow the excess oil to drip away, and transfer to a plate lined with kitchen paper.

Add the fried veal schnitzels to the pan with the tomato sauce, making sure everything is well covered. Cover and cook over moderate heat for about 15 minutes. Make sure the sauce doesn't become too thick. If necessary, add a couple of ladles of hot water. Turn the pieces of meat after 15 minutes and continue simmering for 15 more minutes. Finally, remove the lid and let the sauce cook down slightly, just enough to create a creamy consistency.

PAPPARDELLE SULL'ANATRA
PAPPARDELLE WITH DUCK RAGOUT

My father fondly recounts the following story: When he was little, his nonna would make Pappardelle Sull'anatra, a ragout using duck. On one occasion, my father and his brother were sat at the table with their father and his aunt and uncle, impatiently awaiting the food. Nonna Tina was still at the stove, mixing wide ribbons of pasta with sauce by tossing the pappardelle with a large spoon in the pan—in Italy, the pasta and sauce are always mixed in the pan. Suddenly, all the pappardelle slipped out of the pan and onto the floor! Everyone stared, aghast, at the catastrophe. Nonna Tina shrieked in horror and wanted to throw the pasta away immediately, but that was out of the question. The others scooped up the pasta from the floor and ate it regardless. My father swears it was absolutely delicious!

Pappardelle with duck ragout is a typical Tuscan dish. You can also serve this pasta with ragout made from wild boar, venison, or rabbit. Anyone interested in sampling the cuisine of my homeland should make sure they try this exquisite pasta and ragout.

Serves 6
Preparation: 40 min
Cooking time: 150 min

INGREDIENTS

For the stock:
1 duck carcass (from your local butcher)
1 carrot
1 white onion
1 bay leaf

For the ragout:
1 head celery
1 carrot
1 red onion
Extra-virgin olive oil
1 garlic clove
1 duck (approx. 2 kg / 4.5 lbs), jointed
150 ml (¾ cup) red wine
100 g (½ cup) passata (tomato purée)
1 clove
Salt
Freshly ground black pepper
1 sprig rosemary
1 sprig thyme
2 bay leaves
2 tbsp tomato concentrate (paste)

800 g (1.75 lbs) fresh pappardelle

PREPARATION

To make the stock, place the duck carcass in a large pot, along with the carrot, onion, bay leaf, and 1.5 litres (6 cups) of water, or enough to cover the carcass and vegetables completely. Cover the pot, bring to a boil, and simmer for 40 minutes over low heat.

To make the ragout, peel and finely chop the celery, carrot, and onion. Take a large, wide pan, preferably earthenware, and pour in enough olive oil to cover the base. Place the pan over moderate heat, add the garlic clove and chopped vegetables, and sauté just until the vegetables are soft, being careful to ensure that they do not take on any colour.

Add the pieces of duck (if you like, you can include the giblets, too) and stir. Fry for 1 minute, pour in the wine, and cook until the liquid has evaporated. Then, add the passata and 4 ladles of hot duck stock. Add the clove and season with salt and pepper to taste. Tie the rosemary, thyme, and bay leaves together with kitchen twine and add this to the pan. Bring to a boil briefly, then reduce the temperature to low and simmer for about 90 minutes, stirring occasionally.

At the end of this period, remove the pan from the heat, transfer the pieces of duck to a chopping board, remove the bones, and roughly chop the meat along with the giblets.

Return the chopped duck meat to the pan with the sauce and add the tomato concentrate and 4 ladles of duck stock. Continue simmering for about 60 minutes over low heat. If the sauce becomes too dry, add some more duck stock. Season with salt and pepper.

When the duck ragout is ready, bring a large pan of salted water to a boil, add the pappardelle, and cook it until al dente. Once cooked, drain the pasta, combine it with the duck ragout in a large bowl, and serve immediately.

PESCE

FISH

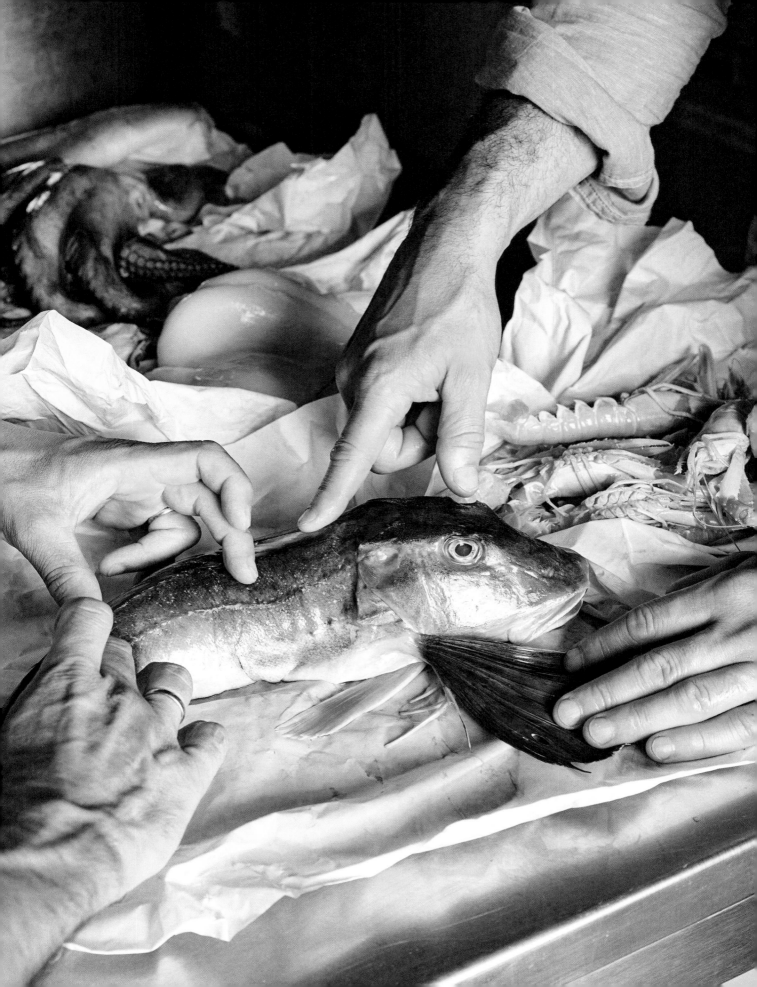

IL PESCIVENDOLO

At the marketplace in Seano, there is an unassuming white market stall with a display of goods of the very highest quality. Not only will you find a remarkable selection of exquisite fish, but you will also be warmly welcomed by the stall vendors, Clara and Piero, who have been married for 32 years. Previously, Piero's family were involved in the fishing trade for many years and ran a fishmonger's shop in Prato. Piero began work there at the age of 13. Eventually, he and his wife decided to give up the shop and dedicate all their energies to running this market stall.

My grandmother Marisa used to buy her fish here, too, not just because of the superb quality, but also because you could always get the best recipe advice. This fish stall does far more than just sell fish. In reality, this is like a fish consultancy centre and a place where people can chat about this and that and catch up on the latest news. Piero's wife, Clara, knows all the customers by name, including their partners and children. She also has all the latest information about recent events like weddings, communions, and birthdays. There is such a welcoming atmosphere here, and the fish—all beautifully presented in the display counter—offer unbeatable inspiration for a delicious supper.

COZZE AL POMODORO
MUSSELS IN TOMATO SAUCE

Whenever I eat cozze al pomodoro, it reminds me of the holiday we took with friends in Sicily when I was nine. There were 30 of us, and we stayed in a house that was right on the beach. One day we bought kilos of mussels, carrying them in giant pans down to the sea to wash them in the salty water. There were loads of children to feed, and this recipe is perfect for such a large group because it is delicious but not too difficult to make. My fondest memory is standing for hours in the water with my siblings, cleaning the mussels and then enjoying the distinctive taste of the ocean when we ate.

Serves 4
Preparation: 20 min
Cooking time: 30–40 min

INGREDIENTS

1 kg (2 lbs) mussels
4 tbsp extra-virgin olive oil, plus more for the bread
2 garlic cloves, peeled
1 bunch parsley
50 ml (3.5 tbsp) white wine
1 small fresh red chilli
400 g (1½ cups) passata (tomato purée)
Salt
Freshly ground black pepper
4 slices of bread

PREPARATION

First, clean the mussels: Rinse them under running water, then scrape off any external impurities using the back of a small knife and remove the beard by tugging it firmly.

Heat 2 tbsp of the oil in a large saucepan and add one whole peeled garlic clove. Fry the garlic just until fragrant, then add the mussels. Set aside some parsley leaves for garnish and add the rest of the bunch whole to the pan. Pour in the white wine, then cover the pan and simmer until the mussels have opened. Switch off the heat.

Meanwhile, seed and finely chop the chilli, and peel and crush the remaining garlic clove.

Heat the remaining 2 tbsp of oil in another saucepan, add the chilli and crushed garlic, and cook over very low heat, stirring occasionally, until the garlic is fragrant. Next, add the passata with a pinch of pepper and salt, but not too much, as the mussels have a strong flavour of their own. Remove the garlic and parsley from the pan with the mussels. Drain the mussels, retaining the stock in a bowl.

Tip the reserved mussel stock into the tomato sauce. Simmer the tomato sauce for another 10 minutes. Next, add the mussels and stir. Finely chop the parsley leaves you set aside earlier, and add them to the mussels and tomato sauce.

Place the bread slices on a baking tray lined with baking paper, drizzle them with oil, then toast under the grill at 250°C/475°F for roughly 3 minutes, until golden.

If desired, sprinkle the mussels liberally with black pepper, then stir them one last time and serve with the slices of toast.

IL CACCIUCCO DI SIMONE

SIMONE'S FISH SOUP

My brother Simone lives in Pisa, close to the sea where they eat a lot of fish. He says all sorts of people there claim to have invented the legendary dish, cacciucco. This popular fish soup is the topic of heated debate in Italy; there are different opinions about the origins of the dish, which is the truly authentic recipe, which version tastes best, and so on. Cacciucco comes in all sorts of varieties in Tuscany. Every family has their own favourite. Our recipe comes from Livorno. Simone swears by this approach because he believes it has such a delicious, fishy flavour. A good cacciucco should always retain the distinct flavour and texture of each fish. In other words, the various kinds of fish should be recognisable, rather than blending into an indeterminate mix. The challenge with this fish soup is getting the different cooking times for each fish correct. The recipe is something for all fish lovers!

Serves 6
Preparation: 20 min
Cooking time: 90 min

INGREDIENTS

1 kg (2 lbs) mussels
680 g (1.5 lbs) octopus
300 g (10 oz) calamari (squid)
850 g (1 lb, 14 oz) gurnard
1 kg (2 lbs) tope
(or soupfin shark) or stargazer
3 garlic cloves
1 white onion
1 small fresh red chilli
5 sage leaves
50 ml (3 tbsp) extra-virgin olive oil
100 ml (½ cup) red wine
200 g (¾ cups) passata
(tomato purée)
400 g (14 oz) king prawns
Salt
Freshly ground black pepper

To serve:
6 slices bread
1 garlic clove, halved
Chopped parsley leaves

TIP

Ask your trusted fishmonger to clean the mussels and fish, as this will save lots of time when preparing this delicious dish. Theoretically, you can use different fish, but they will need to be added in the right sequence and at the right time.

PREPARATION

Clean the mussels and put them in a wide bowl; cover and refrigerate. Clean the octopus, separate the tentacles from the bodies, and chop the tentacles into equal pieces. Clean the squid, slice open the mantle (the main body covering) of the cleaned squid, and cut it into strips. Remove the tail and fins from the gurnard (which should already have been scaled), and split the fish into four equal pieces, retaining the head because it adds flavour to the cacciucco. Cut the tope into equal-size pieces.

Peel the garlic cloves. Finely chop the onion, chilli, and sage leaves, and sauté them in the olive oil with the garlic cloves in a large pan.

Add the chopped octopus, pour in the red wine, and simmer over moderate heat for 30 minutes. There should always be some liquid in the pan, so add hot water if required. Now, add the squid and passata. Cover the pan and simmer over low heat for 30 minutes.

When the fish is almost ready, carefully add the chunks of gurnard and tope; continue cooking for 10–15 minutes with the lid on. Next, add the king prawns and simmer for 5 minutes. Finally, add the mussels, return the lid, and cook for 10 minutes or until the mussels have opened. At this point, taste the cacciucco and add salt and pepper if desired.

To serve, toast the bread under the grill (broiler) in the oven for 5 minutes. Rub the toasted surface of the bread with the cut sides of the halved garlic clove.

Sprinkle the cacciucco with chopped parsley, and serve hot with the toasted bread.

BACCALÀ ALLA LIVORNESE
SALT COD IN TOMATO SAUCE

My mother, Silvia, tells me that her family regularly ate baccalà (salt-preserved cod fillets) served in a sweet tomato sauce. Baccalà is often confused with dried cod. They both involve the same fish, but the preservation method differs. Unlike sun-dried cod, baccalà is cured in salt—this gives it an extremely long shelf life and a highly aromatic flavour. Whenever my bisnonna Zita (my great-grandmother) cooked this dish, it created a wonderful smell throughout the house.

Serves 4
Preparation: 15 min
Cooking time: 30 min

INGREDIENTS

800 g (1.75 lbs) baccalà (salt cod)
or fresh cod with the skin on
50 g (⅓ cup) plain
(all-purpose) flour
1 tbsp extra-virgin olive oil
50 ml (3.5 tbsp) white wine
450 g (1 lb) tinned whole
peeled tomatoes
50 g (1.75 oz) pitted green olives
1 fresh red chilli, finely chopped
1 garlic clove, peeled and crushed
Salt
1 bunch parsley, chopped

TIP

Salt cod (baccalà) can be bought
from Italian, Spanish, and
Portuguese grocers.
If you buy this in larger
quantities, desalt the baccalà as
directed in the recipe, and freeze
the fish so it is ready for use
whenever required. If necessary,
you can also make do with
a simple cod fillet; in that case,
you will need to add a bit more
salt to the tomato sauce.

PREPARATION

To desalt the baccalà: Rinse off the salt under running water, and place the fish in a large bowl of cold water. Leave to soak for 24–36 hours, changing the water every 8 hours, until the fish tastes only slightly salty. The soaking time will depend on the size of the fish.

Chop the desalted baccalà or cod fillet into 4-cm/1½-inch-thick pieces. Put the flour in a bowl and toss the pieces of fish in the flour, shaking off any excess.

Heat the olive oil in a large nonstick pan and fry the floured fish, skin-side down, over moderate heat; turn and continue frying on the other side. Deglaze the pan with the white wine and allow the alcohol to evaporate.

Put the tomatoes in a bowl, crush them with a fork, and add these to the pan with the cod. Add the olives, chilli, garlic, a pinch of salt, and half a glass of water. Cover the pan and cook over low heat for 20 minutes, then remove the lid and simmer for another 5 minutes to allow the sauce to thicken slightly.

Turn off the heat and sprinkle the Baccalà alla Livornese with the chopped parsley to serve.

FRITTO MISTO

FRIED SEAFOOD

Whenever I am at the beach in Tuscany, for example in Viareggio, I consider it my duty to eat fritto misto. I buy it from a barchetta, a boat in the harbour, where it is prepared and sold. Enjoying the sun, sea, and sand with a portion of take-away fish is just part and parcel of the whole experience for me.

When we were kids, we often spent an entire month by the seaside in summer. My parents would cook fritto misto for us at our holiday accommodation. The fish is beautifully crisp on the outside and tender on the inside, with a well-rounded flavour.

Serves 4
Preparation: 15 min
Cooking time: 30-40 min

INGREDIENTS

400 g (14 oz) whole calamari (squid), cleaned (tubes and tentacles separated)
12 red prawns
200 g (7 oz) red mullet fillet (or a different type of fish fillet)
250 g (9 oz) durum wheat semolina
Fine salt
12 fresh anchovies, gutted, heads removed

For frying:
2 litres (8½ cups) groundnut or sunflower oil

To serve:
Juice of 1 lemon

TIP

Note the cooking time for the fish and the temperature of the oil. The temperature should not fall below 180°C/350°F; otherwise, the fried seafood will not be crisp. The bigger the fish, the longer the cooking time.

PREPARATION

Wash the calamari and rinse the prawns and red mullet fillet under running water. Slice the mantle (tube) of the calamari into rings. Depending on your preference, you might want to chop the fish into bite-size pieces.

In a deep pot, heat the oil to 180°C/350°F. Preheat the oven to 100°C/210°F.

Put the semolina in a bowl. Lightly season the calamari rings and tentacles with salt, then mix well with the semolina in the bowl. Transfer to a sieve and shake off the excess semolina over a bowl. Fry the calamari rings and tentacles in 4 portions, one after the other, for roughly 1 minute each. Remove with a slotted spoon, drain on kitchen paper, and keep warm in a dish in the preheated oven.

Toss the prawns in the semolina, then fry for about 1 minute, until golden brown. Drain and add to the calamari to keep warm in the oven.

Lightly season the anchovies and red mullet fillet with salt, then toss them in the semolina. Transfer to a sieve and shake off the excess semolina. Fry in the hot oil for about 30 seconds, until cooked through. Remove with a slotted spoon and drain on kitchen paper.

Serve all the seafood on a platter, and drizzle with lemon juice to taste.

CALAMARI RIPIENI

STUFFED CALAMARI

Calamari (squid) are the perfect shape for stuffing, and their mild flavour provides an excellent pairing with a filling made of breadcrumbs, parsley, garlic, lemon zest, and the calamari tentacles themselves. This wonderful dish has a fresh, summery taste.

Serves 4
Preparation: 15 min
Cooking time: 20–30 min

INGREDIENTS

700 g (1.5 lbs) calamari (squid)
4 tbsp extra-virgin olive oil, divided
Dried chilli flakes

For the filling:
1 bunch parsley
10 basil leaves
2 garlic cloves, divided
15 pitted black olives
50 g (1.75 oz) grated scamorza (Italian cheese)
2 tbsp breadcrumbs
Zest of 1 lemon
1 egg, beaten
Salt
Freshly ground black pepper
50 ml (3.5 tbsp) white wine
200 g (7 oz) plum tomatoes, halved
50 g (¼ cups) passata (tomato purée)

PREPARATION

Clean the calamari by removing the ink sac, eyes, and outer skin, and chop the tentacles (or ask your fishmonger to clean the calamari when you buy them).

Sauté the chopped tentacles in a pan with 2 tbsp of the olive oil and the chilli until they are firm.

Carefully wash the parsley and basil and drain well. Finely chop the parsley, basil, one of the garlic cloves, and the olives. Set aside some chopped parsley for the garnish.

In a wide bowl, combine the chopped ingredients, tentacles, scamorza, breadcrumbs, the egg, and lemon zest, and season with salt and pepper, making sure everything is mixed well. Stuff the calamari mantles (tubes) with this mixture. Do not add too much, or the filling may spill out during the cooking process. Seal the open ends of the calamari with toothpicks.

Heat the remaining 2 tbsp of oil in a wide, high-sided saucepan or skillet and sauté the second garlic clove until fragrant. Add the stuffed calamari and fry on both sides, then pour in the white wine. Add the halved plum tomatoes and the passata, cover the pan, and simmer for 10 minutes or until the stuffing is firm. Transfer the stuffed calamari to a serving plate, sprinkle with the rest of the chopped parsley, and serve warm.

BRANZINO AL CARTOCCIO IN FOGLIE DI FICO
SEA BASS WRAPPED IN FIG LEAVE

The inspiration for this recipe came from the enormous fig tree that grows next to Poggianella. The fish is stuffed with figs and takes on an exquisite flavour, which is simultaneously sweet and savoury. A delicious summer dish.

Serves 4
Preparation: 15 min
Baking time: 20–30 min

INGREDIENTS

10 fresh figs
8–10 fig leaves (alternatively, chestnut leaves)
300 g (10 oz) sea bass, gutted
Salt
1 lemon, sliced
2 sprigs dill
2 tbsp extra-virgin olive oil

TIP

You can order fig leaves online or use leaves from a chestnut tree. A delicious sauce can be conjured up from a couple of roasted figs: Just use a hand blender to purée the figs with some fresh dill, olive oil, lemon juice, and salt.

PREPARATION

Preheat the oven to 200°C/400°F (non-fan setting). Line a baking tray with baking paper.

Wash and dry the figs and fig leaves, cut the figs in half, and set both aside.

Wash the gutted fish under running water and season with salt, both inside and outside. Stuff the belly of the fish with a slice of lemon, the halved figs, and a sprig of dill. Next, lay 4–5 fig leaves in a line on a chopping board, overlapping them slightly, and position the fish on top. Place one sprig of dill on top of the fish and wrap everything up, using kitchen twine to tie the parcel securely.

Place the fig leaf parcel on the prepared baking tray and drizzle with oil. Bake for 20–30 minutes. Remove the parcel from the oven, peel away the fig leaves, and arrange the fish on a plate with the cooked figs, remaining slices of lemon, and the remaining fig leaves.

INSALATA DI LEGUMI E MOSCARDINI

BEAN SALAD WITH BABY OCTOPUS

This salad with baby octopus and beans is my own creation. Moscardini (a small kind of octopus) are a regional Italian speciality. They are mainly found in the Mediterranean area, with most of this fishing taking place in Liguria, using environmentally friendly methods to avoid damaging the ecosystem. In Italy, you can buy fresh or frozen moscardini, which measure about 10 cm (4 inches) in length. Here, I combine them with beans and chickpeas, which are common and popular ingredients in Tuscany. These legumes are nutritious (high protein content) and very healthy (high vitamin and mineral content). I particularly like the taste of chickpeas and beans; I prefer the freshly prepared variety, rather than tinned, as the former have a better texture and more flavour. With the addition of baby octopus and salad ingredients, you have a fresh, summer dish that also looks exquisite on the plate.

Serves 4
Preparation: 15 min
Soaking and cooking time:
depends on the types of
legumes

INGREDIENTS

50 g (1.75 oz) dried chickpeas
(garbanzo beans) (or tinned)
50 g (1.75 oz) dried
black-eyed beans/peas
(or tinned)
50 g (1.75 oz) dried cannellini
beans (or tinned)
1 bay leaf
1 garlic clove, peeled
Salt

1 kg (2 lbs) moscardini (baby
octopus) or calamari (squid)
400 g (14 oz) colourful cherry
tomatoes
1 small fresh red chilli
50 g (1.75 oz) pitted black olives
Leaves from 1 sprig thyme
Leaves from 1 bunch basil

For the dressing:
3 tbsp extra-virgin olive oil
Zest of 1 lemon
Juice of ½ lemon
1 tbsp white wine vinegar
½ garlic clove, grated
Salt
Freshly ground black pepper

PREPARATION

Soak all the dried beans in water the night before, following the instructions on the pack. The next morning, drain and rinse them under running water. Fill a saucepan with 1 litre (4¼ cups) of water and add the bay leaf, garlic clove, and all the soaked pulses. Bring to a boil and cook over moderate heat, salting the mixture after about 50 minutes. Simmer for roughly another 10 minutes, until the beans and chickpeas are soft. Drain well and leave to cool. (If you are using tinned beans, skip this step. Instead, drain and rinse the beans under cool running water and set aside.)

To clean the baby octopus, remove the eyes and beak, and wash away any sand under running water, making sure to clean inside the folds, too. Then, add the octopus to a pan of boiling water and cook for about 20 minutes over moderate heat, until tender. The cooking time will depend on the size of the octopus, so adjust accordingly. Once the octopus is cooked, drain it well and leave to cool, then chop it into bite-size pieces.

Meanwhile, wash and drain the cherry tomatoes and fresh chilli. Halve the cherry tomatoes, and slice the chilli into thin rings. Set aside.

Make the dressing in a small dish by whisking together the olive oil, lemon zest, lemon juice, white wine vinegar, and grated garlic with a fork until you have a smooth emulsion. Season to taste with salt and pepper; set aside.

As soon as the ingredients are cool, prepare the salad: In a large bowl, combine the beans, chopped baby octopus, tomatoes, sliced chilli, olives, and chopped thyme and basil. Add the dressing and toss well. Cover and refrigerate for at least 2 hours to allow the flavours to infuse. Serve cold.

PASTA ALLE VONGOLE
PASTA WITH CLAMS

My grandmother, Nonna Marisa, got this recipe from the fish stall in Seano, which is now run by Piero and Clara (p. 42). Nonna Marisa was very fond of seafood, so she regularly made this pasta for special occasions—for example, for visitors or on Sundays or holidays.

Serves 4
Preparation: 45 min
Cooking time: 30 min
Time to make in advance: 2 hrs

INGREDIENTS
400 g (14 oz) clams
2 bunches flat-leaf parsley, plus extra for the garnish
3 tbsp extra-virgin olive oil
2 garlic cloves, peeled
200 ml (¾ cup) dry white wine
300 g (10.5 oz) cherry tomatoes
450 g (1 lb) spaghetti di grano duro (durum wheat spaghetti)
Pinch of saffron threads
1 fresh red chilli, chopped
Salt
Freshly ground black pepper

TIP
Cook a few parsley stalks with the clams, as they impart lots of flavour.

PREPARATION
Check the clams individually and remove any with broken shells. Soak the clams in cold water for at least 2 hours, changing the water 2 or 3 times and removing the sand.

Wash the parsley and dab it dry with a cloth. Strip the leaves from the stalks of one bunch of parsley, chop them finely, and set both the stalks and chopped leaves aside. Chop the leaves from the second bunch of parsley and discard the stems.

Heat the olive oil in a large frying pan. As soon as it is hot, add one garlic clove, the reserved parsley stalks, and the clams. After a couple of minutes, pour in the white wine, cover the pan, and wait until the clams have completely opened, 3–4 minutes. Remove all but one-third of the clams from their shells. Discard the empty shells.

Strain the cooking liquid into a saucepan through a fine sieve, bring this to a boil with the lid on but slightly open, then remove from the heat and set aside.

Halve the cherry tomatoes, chop the second clove of garlic, and add both to the frying pan you used to cook the clams. Sauté until the garlic is fragrant, then add roughly ½ cup of the clam cooking liquid and simmer for 3 minutes.

Bring a large pot of water to a boil and add the spaghetti. About halfway through the cooking time recommended on the package, remove the spaghetti from the boiling water (important: do not throw away the water!) and add it to the frying pan with the cherry tomatoes and garlic. With a ladle, gradually add roughly 1 litre (4¼ cups) of the pasta water and about two-thirds of the warm clam broth to the frying pan.

Pour a few tablespoons of the remaining clam broth into a small bowl, drop in the saffron, and let it soak for a minute or two.

Stir the saffron mixture into the spaghetti, along with the chopped chilli and salt to taste, and let the pasta cook, stirring regularly and adding more of the clam broth if required, until al dente. This cooking method will result in a creamy sauce.

When the spaghetti is al dente, turn off the heat, add the shelled clams and the rest of the chopped parsley, and adjust the seasonings with salt and pepper if desired.

Arrange the spaghetti on a plate with the clams that are still in their shells. Scatter with a handful of chopped parsley to serve.

INSALATA POLPO E PATATE

OCTOPUS AND POTATO SALAD

Octopus and potato salad is very popular in Italy. Originally, this salad is said to have come from Sicily, but nowadays you will find it in lots of places along the Italian coast. I have known this dish my entire life, but I can't tell you exactly where from. It wasn't something we made at home, though we certainly ate it on our summer holidays. These days, I make this salad very frequently—the fresh taste produced by the combination of octopus and potatoes never fails to impress guests. You need a good quality oil, waxy potatoes, and, of course, you must make sure you cook the octopus for the correct length of time so it is tender rather than chewy. If you follow those rules, this will be an irresistible and incredibly delicious dish.

Serves 8
Preparation: 20 min
Cooking time: 40–60 min
Resting time: 60 min

INGREDIENTS

1 kg (2 lbs) octopus (whole, fresh or frozen)

For the stock:
1 sprig parsley
Whole black peppercorns
2 garlic cloves, peeled
100 ml (½ cup) white wine
1 tsp salt

For the salad:
600 g (1.3 lbs) waxy potatoes
2 sprigs parsley, chopped
Zest of 1 lemon
1 garlic clove, finely chopped
Pinch of salt
100 g (3.5 oz) sun-dried tomatoes, chopped
50 g (1.75 oz) pitted black olives
3 tsp capers
1 small fresh red chilli (optional), chopped

For the dressing:
Juice of 1 lemon
1 tbsp white wine vinegar
3 tbsp extra-virgin olive oil
Salt
Freshly ground black pepper

PREPARATION

If you are using frozen octopus, defrost it overnight in the fridge.

Clean the fresh octopus by removing the eyes and beak. Then, place it in a bowl and vigorously rub the tentacles together under running water to ensure that all impurities are gradually removed from the suction pads and the skin is no longer slimy.

To make the stock, put 3 litres (12½ cups) of water in large pot and add the parsley sprig, a couple of black peppercorns, the garlic, white wine, and salt. Bring to a boil. Add the octopus to the stock, cover with a lid, and cook over moderate heat for about 40 minutes. Allow a cooking time of 40 minutes per kilo of octopus. Test with a fork to see if it is done. It should feel soft and easily penetrable when you insert the prongs. Remove the pot from the heat, and leave the octopus to cool in the cooking water. Then, drain and leave the octopus in a sieve for at least 30 minutes to allow the skin to dry out slightly.

To make the salad, boil the potatoes in their skins until cooked. Drain the potatoes and leave them to cool, then peel and chop them into small chunks.

Put the potatoes in a large bowl, along with all but a few tbsp of the chopped parsley, the lemon zest, chopped garlic, salt, chopped dried tomatoes, black olives, capers, and chilli (if using).

Chop the octopus into bite-size pieces and add it to the bowl.

To make the dressing, whisk together the lemon juice, vinegar, oil, and salt and pepper to taste. Pour the dressing over the salad, mix well, and leave the flavours to infuse for 1 hour in the refrigerator. Sprinkle with the remaining chopped parsley before serving.

SOGLIOLA AL CARTOCCIO
SOLE BAKED IN PARCELS

Sogliola al Cartoccio is a dish my mother makes when she is in a hurry. It is an easy recipe that wasn't regarded as particularly special at our house—just a simple Friday fish supper, which is greatly underappreciated, in my view. The fish and vegetables are sealed in a baking paper parcel and cooked together. This technique allows the fish to absorb all the flavours sealed within the parcel as it cooks. The result is a light and delicious dish.

Serves 4
Preparation: 15 min
Baking time: 15–20 min

INGREDIENTS
4 skinless sole or plaice fillets
(approx. 200 g / 7 oz each)
2 lemons, sliced
2 garlic cloves, sliced
4 sprigs rosemary
Leaves from 2 sprigs thyme,
chopped
4 tbsp extra-virgin olive oil
10 cherry tomatoes
Salt
Freshly ground black pepper

TIP
You can replace the rosemary
and thyme with other herbs, such
as fresh parsley or tarragon.

PREPARATION
Preheat the oven to 200°C/400°F (non-fan setting).

For each sole fillet, place a large square of baking paper on the work surface. In the centre of each sheet, put 2–3 slices of lemon (depending on the size of the fish), a few slices of garlic, and a sprig of rosemary. Put the sole on top and sprinkle with chopped thyme and a pinch of salt and pepper. Brush with 1 tbsp oil and place a few cherry tomatoes on the fish. Wrap everything in the baking paper, and firmly seal the parcel to ensure that the steam does not escape during cooking.

Place the parcels on a baking tray and bake for 15–20 minutes. Remove from the oven, and allow to rest for 3–4 minutes before opening. Serve hot.

DESSERTS

ANTONIO MATTEI BISCOTTIFICIO

If you visit Prato today, you will still find the biscuit factory that was founded there by Antonio Mattei in the 19th century, where the world-famous cantucci are made. This factory is now owned by my former babysitter Elisabetta, who used to change my nappies and feed me pasta. A little bakery here makes the famous almond biscuits and other treats, which are then sold in Italy, Germany, France, northern Europe, the USA, Canada, and China.

Elisabetta Pandolfini is the third generation to run this company. Her family took over the biscottificio from Antonio Mattei. Elisabetta's grandfather Ernesto began working there at the age of 12, and he took over the business in 1908. He continued the tradition of making cantucci biscuits, as well as selling his own specialities that are still classics today.

Products from the bakery come packed in a dark blue bag and have become a symbol of the city of Prato. Indeed, the manufacturing facilities are now a tourist attraction. But it certainly isn't just tourists who shop here; the products are much appreciated by Prato's residents, too. My family regularly has a blue Antonio Mattei bag in the kitchen. The company continues to offer exceptional quality, and the products are traditionally Tuscan. More information can be found at www.antoniomattei.it.

LINGUE DI GATTO
CAT TONGUE BISCUITS

My nonna Marisa always bought these biscuits from a well-known pasticceria in Prato and served them with creamy gelato. I think "cat tongue" biscuits go brilliantly with a cup of coffee and Zabaione (p. 181). I could wolf these down by the tonne. In fact, the time I most often make them is if we have friends coming over and I want something to serve at the end of an evening meal. The biscuits are incredibly quick and easy to make, and you only need four ingredients.

Serves 4 (approx. 30 biscuits)
Preparation: 30 min
Resting time: 15 min
Baking time: 15 min

INGREDIENTS

50 g (3½ tbsp) butter
50 g (1.75 oz) egg white
(approx. 1 egg)
60 g (⅓ cup) icing
(powdered) sugar
50 g (⅓ cup) plain
(all-purpose) flour

PREPARATION

Leave the butter to soften at room temperature in a bowl.

Use a hand mixer to whisk the egg white until it holds its shape.

Sift the icing sugar over the butter, and stir with a spatula to create a smooth and fluffy mixture. Sift in half the flour and stir to combine, then fold in half the whisked egg white. Once everything is combined, sift in the remaining flour, then fold in the rest of the whisked egg white. Stir carefully until you have a smooth and creamy consistency.

Transfer this mixture to a piping bag with a plain nozzle and chill in the fridge for at least 15 minutes.

Meanwhile, heat the oven to 190°C/375°F (non-fan setting). Line a baking tray with baking paper.

Pipe 7–8-cm-/2.75–3-inch-long strips of the mixture on the prepared baking tray, leaving gaps of at least 3 cm/1 inch, then bake for about 15 minutes. As soon as they are golden around the edges, remove the biscuits from the oven and immediately lift them off the tray with the help of a spatula. Leave to cool completely before serving.

CENCI
FRIED PASTRY STRIPS

These carnival pastries come from my home city of Prato. The word cenci means "shreds" or "rags" and is a reference to the fabric remnants from the textile factories for which Prato is known. The leftover fabric is torn into ragged scraps to be used in various ways. These biscuits are inspired by the shape of those pieces of fabric or rags.

Cenci keep for a long while, and it is said they are usually made by patient Tuscan grandmothers because they take a bit of time. I like to make them in bulk and keep them in a biscuit tin or jar. Cenci and a cup of coffee are a lovely way to round off an evening meal with friends.

Serves 8
Preparation: 20 min
Resting time: 30 min

INGREDIENTS

250 g (2 cups) plain
(all-purpose) flour
20 g (1 tbsp plus 1 tsp) caster
(superfine) sugar
2 eggs
Zest of 1 lemon
Zest of 1 orange
20 g (1½ tbsp) butter, melted
2 tbsp vin santo (Italian
dessert wine; alternatively, use
marsala wine)
Pinch of salt
30 g (¼ cup) icing (powdered)
sugar, for dusting

For frying:
1 litre (4¼ cups) groundnut or
sunflower oil

TIP

To keep the cenci crisp, store
them in an airtight container.

PREPARATION

Sift the flour into a mound on a large work surface, and create a well in the centre. Put the sugar, eggs, lemon zest, orange zest, melted butter, vin santo, and salt in this recess. Work the mixture together by hand until the texture is very elastic and smooth and no longer sticking to your hands. Wrap the biscuit dough in a kitchen towel and leave to rest for 30 minutes at room temperature.

Use a rolling pin to roll out the dough until it is very thin (approx. 2 mm), and use a knife or cutting wheel to cut it into 3-cm/1-inch-wide strips. Create indentations with a fork along the edges of each strip of dough.

Heat the oil in a large frying pan (the base should be well-covered) to a temperature of 180°C/350°F. Fry the strips of biscuit dough in batches for about 30 seconds per side, keeping a constant eye on them and turning them with tongs.

Carefully remove the cenci from the oil, and drain them for a few minutes on a rack covered with kitchen paper. Dust with icing sugar before serving.

ZABAIONE
ITALIAN CUSTARD

For several years, my family lived in a sleepy little village in the mountains of Austria. Our neighbours had a farm with pigs, cows, and chickens. We would go there every day to buy fresh milk, but also delicious eggs that were perfect for rustling up wonderful zabaione.

My father always mixes his zabaione with the end of his coffee in the cup to create his very own variation on this dessert. This involves stirring the zabaione for a good while with a spoon until it turns slightly brown, at which point he eats it. Nowadays, I also like to mix in a small amount of coffee—it makes an excellent combination. Zabaione also goes beautifully with Lingue di Gatto (p. 173).

Serves 4
Preparation: 15 minutes
Cooking time: 10 minutes

INGREDIENTS
Ice cubes
5 tbsp vin santo (Italian dessert wine; alternatively, use marsala wine)
28 g (¼ cup) caster (superfine) sugar
6 egg yolks

TIP
Coffee-lovers can follow my father's example and mix in a couple of teaspoons of brewed coffee to taste.

PREPARATION

Fill a large bowl with ice cubes and place it in the freezer.

Pour the vin santo into a small saucepan, add half the sugar, and warm over low heat just until the sugar dissolves; turn off the heat. The vin santo should not be heated too much; otherwise, the alcohol will evaporate. Do not exceed a temperature of 35°C/95°F (check with a kitchen thermometer).

Heat water for a bain-marie in a second saucepan. Use only an inch or two of water, so the bottom of the mixing bowl does not touch the water in the next step and the pot does not overflow.

Put the egg yolks in a heat-resistant mixing bowl and beat with a balloon whisk, adding the rest of the sugar and continuing to whisk until you have a smooth mixture. Then, add 2 tbsp of the warm vin santo to thin out the mixture. Set the bowl over simmering water in the second saucepan.

Swiftly add the remaining 3 tbsp of warm Vin Santo, stirring it in with the balloon whisk, and continue whisking the mixture constantly over the bain-marie. The mixture will gradually thicken and the foam will disappear.

Keep stirring constantly until the creamy mixture increases in volume; the balloon whisk should leave a distinct trace. The temperature of the mixture will now be roughly 83°C/181°F. When you lift the balloon whisk, the mixture should adhere to the wires and not drop off.

Take the bowl of ice cubes out of the freezer. Transfer the zabaione to a wide dish or pie plate that will fit inside the bowl, and place this on top of the ice cubes in the bowl. Use a spatula to continue stirring everything gently for a few minutes. This technique ensures that the zabaione cools quickly while retaining its light and airy consistency, and doesn't form a skin.

Transfer the creamy custard into little bowls to serve.

TORTA DELLA NONNA
ITALIAN CUSTARD TART

Torta della Nonna, "Granny's tart," is a simple recipe consisting of crema pasticcera (pastry cream), pine nuts, and shortcrust pastry—and it is particularly popular in my family. My sister-in-law Noemi is an outstanding baker, since her uncle is a well-known pastry chef in Calabria who has taught her well. On special occasions, she treats us all to her Torta della Nonna.

Serves 10
Preparation: 50 min
Baking time: 50–60 min

INGREDIENTS

For the crema pasticcera
(pastry cream):
1 vanilla pod
500 ml (2 cups) whole milk
125 g (4 oz) egg yolk
(from approx. 7 eggs)
100 g (½ cup) caster
(superfine) sugar
40 g (⅓ cup) cornflour
(cornstarch)

For the shortcrust:
450 g (3½ cups) Italian 00 flour
200 g (7 oz) cold butter
160 g (¾ cup) caster
(superfine) sugar
2 medium eggs
Zest of 1 lemon

For the topping
Egg white, beaten
30 g (1 oz) pine nuts
2 tsp icing (powdered) sugar

PREPARATION

To make the crema pasticcera, slice the vanilla pod lengthwise and scrape out the seeds. Put the milk, vanilla seeds, and pod in a medium saucepan and bring to a boil. Remove the pan from the heat, cover, and leave to infuse. Meanwhile, whisk the egg yolks in a large bowl with the sugar until you have a pale, thick, and creamy mixture. Add the cornflour and continue whisking until smooth.

Remove the vanilla pod from the milk. Slowly, pour one-third of the warm milk into the egg yolk mixture in the bowl, stirring constantly with a balloon whisk. The egg yolks should slowly adjust to the higher temperature. Now, put the egg mixture in the pan with the rest of the warm milk, and stir constantly over moderate heat until it thickens. It is essential to keep stirring while the mixture cooks; otherwise, there is a risk that it will catch on the base of the pan, resulting in lumps. To make shortcrust pastry, put the flour in a bowl with the chunks of cold butter. Rub the butter with your fingertips, mixing it well with the flour until you have a sandy texture. Tip this mixture out onto the work surface, and create a well in the centre. Put the sugar, eggs, and lemon zest in the well and work the ingredients together briefly—just sufficiently to bring the mixture together and shape it into a ball. Wrap the pastry in clingfilm or a tea towel, and leave to rest in the fridge for at least 30 minutes.

Preheat the oven to 180°C/350°F (non-fan setting).

Grease and flour a 26-cm/10-inch-diameter tart tin. Use a rolling pin to roll out half the pastry on a lightly floured work surface to a thickness of 2–3 mm, and carefully transfer it to the prepared tin. Press the pastry into place with your fingers, making sure it sticks to the base and high up the sides. Trim any excess pastry. Prick the base in several places with a fork, and spread with the cold crema pasticcera.

Work the remaining shortcrust together once more, and roll it out to a thickness of 2–3 mm. Drape the pastry over the rolling pin and transfer it to the tin, smoothing it out over the top of the pastry cream while applying slight pressure so any excess pastry can be trimmed away around the edges. This creates the lid. Carefully prick the surface in several places with a moistened fork. Lightly brush the top with the beaten egg white and sprinkle with pine nuts.

Bake on the lowest shelf in the oven for about 15 minutes, then lower the temperature to 160°C/320°F and continue cooking for 45 minutes. At the end of this baking time, remove the tart from the oven and leave to cool for 4 hours. Sprinkle with icing sugar to serve.

SCHIACCIATA CON'UVA

YEASTED GRAPE CAKE

This light cake has a sweet and fruity flavour with a hint of spicy aniseed, and it is an important dish from my childhood. Whenever this cake appeared, it meant it was harvest time; at Poggianella, we harvested our own grapes and used them to make this cake. Traditionally, schiacciata con'uva is baked in autumn when October brings us dark, sweet grapes ready for winemaking. It tastes best with Cannaiolo grapes from the Chianti region. These give the dough a pale purple tinge and add the necessary sweetness, as the dough itself is not particularly sweet. The dough is the same as Tuscan bread, so Schiacciata con'uva is essentially a flatbread with grapes. My sister Maria Rachele loves making this "grape bread," and her version is excellent. During the two months when Cannaiolo grapes are available, she bakes this cake at every opportunity.

Serves 8
Preparation: 20 min
Resting time: 120 min
Baking time: 40–50 min

INGREDIENTS

400 g (3¼ cups) plain
(all-purpose) flour
Pinch of salt
170 g (¾ cup plus 1 tbsp) caster
(superfine) sugar, divided
20 g (0.7 oz) fresh brewer's yeast
Lukewarm water
3 tbsp extra-virgin olive oil
1 kg (2 lbs) black or red
seedless grapes
4 tsp aniseed

For the rosemary oil:
8 tbsp extra-virgin olive oil
2 sprigs rosemary

PREPARATION

In a bowl, combine the flour with the salt and 2 tbsp of the sugar, mound the mixture on a work surface, and make a well in the top. Dissolve the yeast in a couple tbsp of lukewarm water in a glass, then pour the mixture into the mound of flour, along with the olive oil.

Knead by hand, gradually adding spoonfuls of lukewarm water until you have a smooth, stretchy dough that is no longer sticky. Shape this into a ball, transfer to a bowl, cover with a cloth, and leave to prove for 2 hours or until doubled in volume.

To make the rosemary oil, heat the olive oil in a small pan. As soon as it is warm, pour it into a bowl and add the sprigs of rosemary. Set aside and leave to cool.

Remove all the grapes from the stalks, then wash and drain them well. Put the grapes in a wide dish and toss with 130 g/⅔ cup sugar and 5 tbsp of the rosemary oil until well combined.

Preheat the oven to 180°C/350°F (non-fan setting). Line a baking tray with baking paper or coat it with oil.

Knead the dough again at the end of the proving period, and divide it into two equal pieces. Roll out one half on a floured surface to create a thin sheet, then transfer to the prepared baking tray. Cover the dough with two-thirds of the grapes, and sprinkle with half the aniseed.

Roll the second half of dough into a thin sheet and place this over the first half on the tray, completely covering the grapes. Press the edges of the dough firmly together. Press down with both hands on the surface of the dough so that the grapes underneath release their juices.

Scatter the remaining grapes over the top, sprinkle with 2 tbsp of sugar and aniseed, then drizzle with the remaining rosemary oil.

Bake for 30–40 minutes, until golden. Halfway through the cooking time, cover the surface with aluminium foil. Leave to cool before eating.

BIANCO E NERO DELLA NONNA MARISA

NONNA MARISA'S MARBLE CAKE

At Easter, we always had a huge homemade chocolate egg. Nonna Marisa, my mother's mother, would use any leftover chocolate to make this cake. Everyone loved it so much, we would get a bigger and bigger egg every year so that the leftovers could be used to make an even bigger cake. Eventually, my granny would buy chocolate especially for the purpose of making this cake, and this became part of our Easter tradition. The next day for breakfast, we always ate leftover cake dunked in a glass of milk.

Serves 8
Preparation: 20 min
Baking time: 35 min

INGREDIENTS

250 g (9 oz) butter
200 g (7 oz) dark chocolate
4 eggs
200 g (1 cup) caster
(superfine) sugar
250 ml (1 cup) whole milk
Salt
450 g (3½ cups) Italian 00 flour
3 tsp baking powder
2 tsp icing (powdered) sugar,
for dusting

TIP

My granny used to insert whole pieces of chocolate between the two layers, which you would then rediscover when enjoying the cooled cake!

PREPARATION

Melt the butter in a small pan over low heat, then leave to cool.

Melt the dark chocolate in a heatproof bowl over a pan of simmering water (bain-marie), then set aside.

Preheat the oven to 180°C/350°F (non-fan setting).

Beat the eggs in a large bowl and add the sugar. Use a balloon whisk to beat the ingredients until the mixture is frothy and has doubled in volume. Add the milk, melted butter, and a pinch of salt and stir.

In a separate bowl, combine the sifted flour and baking powder, then gradually add this to the bowl with the egg mixture, stirring well until you have a smooth batter.

Grease a 30 × 40-cm (12 × 16-inch) cake tin, then dust with flour, shaking out any excess. Put half the cake batter into the tin.

Stir the melted dark chocolate into the other half of the cake mix, combining well. Spread the chocolatey cake mix over the plain mix in the tin, then swirl a fork in spirals through both layers to allow the two colours to mingle.

Bake in the centre of the oven for about 35 minutes. Remove from the oven, leave to cool completely, and dust with icing sugar before serving.

ZUPPA INGLESE
WHITE AND BLACK TRIFLE

Zuppa Inglese, which means English soup, is another dish for using up leftovers—in this case crema pasticcera (pastry cream), which forms the basis of lots of sweet recipes in Italy. In Italian cuisine, the role played by crema pasticcera in desserts is similar to that played by tomato sauce in savoury dishes. Whenever we have any extra pastry cream, my sister Elisabetta makes the finest zuppa Inglese I have ever tasted, much to the delight of the entire family. Nonna Tina also liked making this dessert and always decorated it with a couple of coffee beans to give the crema a subtle coffee flavour.

Serves 12
Preparation: 35 min
Resting time: 2 hrs in the fridge

INGREDIENTS
For the crema pasticcera
(pastry cream):
½ vanilla pod
1 litre (4¼ cups) whole milk
12 egg yolks
430 g (2 cups plus 2 tbsp) caster
(superfine) sugar
80 g (⅔ cups) cornflour
(cornstarch)
30 g (1 oz) unsweetened cocoa
powder

For the syrup:
170 ml (¾ cup) water
80 g (⅓ cup plus 2 scant tbsp)
caster (superfine) sugar
250 g (1 cup) alchermes
(Italian liqueur)
30 large, soft sponge fingers

PREPARATION
To make the crema pasticcera: Scrape out the seeds from the vanilla pod half. Put the milk, vanilla seeds, and pod in a pan and bring to a boil. Remove the pan from the heat, cover, and leave to infuse.

Meanwhile, whisk the egg yolks in a bowl with the sugar until you have a pale, thick, and creamy mixture. Add the cornflour and continue whisking until smooth. Remove the vanilla pod from the milk. Slowly pour one-third of the warm milk into the egg yolk mixture in the bowl, stirring constantly with a balloon whisk. The egg yolks should slowly adjust to the higher temperature.

Now, put the egg mixture in the pan with the rest of the warm milk, and stir constantly over a moderate heat until it thickens. It is essential to keep stirring while the mixture cooks; otherwise, there is a risk that it will catch on the base of the pan, resulting in lumps.

Divide the crema pasticcera between two bowls. Sprinkle one bowl with a pinch of sugar to prevent a skin from forming on the surface. Sift the cocoa over the other bowl and fold it in. Leave both bowls of crema pasticcera to cool.

To make the syrup, put the water and sugar in a small saucepan, bring to a boil, and switch off the heat. Add the alchermes and stir it in. Pour the syrup into a shallow dish.

Briefly dunk the sponge fingers in the syrup on both sides so they change colour but do not get too soggy (roughly 2 seconds per side). Line the base of a glass bowl (approx. 20 cm/8 inches wide and 7–8 cm/3 inches tall) with sponge fingers, then cover with some of the chocolate cream. Continue with the rest of the soaked sponge fingers, adding alternate layers of plain crema pasticcera and chocolate cream. The top layer should consist of plain crema pasticcera.

Cover and chill for at least 2 hours to allow the flavours to develop before serving.

LE CIAMBELLE DI ELISABETTA
ELISABETTA'S FRIED ITALIAN DOUGHNUTS

My sister Elisabetta regularly makes ciambelle for us on a grand scale. She stands in the kitchen for hours, patiently frying these sweet pastries. My family had a special tradition of making ciambelle for my sister Ester's birthday. We would always place bets on who could eat the most. If there happened to be any leftovers, we would eat them for breakfast the next day with a drink of milk. These doughnuts are delicious, whatever the occasion.

Makes 20 doughnuts
Preparation: 40 min
Resting time: 90 min

INGREDIENTS

7 g (0.25 oz) active dried yeast
60 g (⅓ cup) plus 1 tsp caster (superfine) sugar
550 g (1.2 lbs) Manitoba flour
200 ml (1 cup) whole milk, lukewarm
80 g (5 tbsp) butter, melted
2 eggs
Zest of one orange
4 tbsp rum
Seeds from 1 vanilla pod

For frying:
1 litre (4¼ cups) groundnut or sunflower oil

To serve:
Caster (superfine) sugar

TIP

You can also bake these doughnuts in a preheated oven for about 20 minutes at 170–180°C/340–350°F (non-fan setting).

PREPARATION

Quickly combine the yeast with 1 tsp sugar in a wide bowl, then add the flour and combine well by hand.

In a second large bowl, mix the lukewarm milk with the remaining sugar, butter, eggs, grated orange zest, rum, and vanilla seeds.

Gradually mix the flour and yeast mixture into the milk mixture until you have a firm dough. Transfer the dough to a floured work surface, and continue kneading until it is soft and stretchy and can be shaped into a ball—this takes about 10 minutes.

Put the dough in a bowl that has been dusted with flour, cover with a kitchen towel, and leave to prove in an unheated oven with the light switched on (the temperature should be roughly 28°C/82°F) for about 2 hours, until it has doubled in volume.

Tip the dough out onto the floured work surface, then knead it again. Use a rolling pin to roll the dough out to a thickness of about 2 cm (¾ inch).

Stamp out circles of dough using an 8-cm/3-inch cutter, and make a 2-cm/¾-inch hole in the centre of each (if you don't have suitable cutters, use a glass). Place the doughnut rings on a sheet of baking paper, spaced out with gaps of about 3 cm/1 inch. Cover with a kitchen towel and leave to prove for another 20–30 minutes.

Cut the baking paper underneath the rings of dough into squares, so each ring gets its own square.

Heat the oil in a deep pan. Make sure the temperature does not exceed 170°C/340°F; otherwise, the dough can cook too quickly and brown on the outside while failing to cook all the way through. Use a kitchen thermometer if necessary.

Transfer the dough rings on the baking paper into the hot oil. Once the baking paper is immersed in hot oil, carefully peel it away from one corner using kitchen tongs. Fry the rings for about 3 minutes, until golden. Use a slotted spoon to scoop the doughnuts out of the oil and transfer them to a wire rack lined with kitchen paper to drain. Sprinkle with sugar while still warm, and transfer to a serving plate. Leave to cool briefly before serving.

CIAMBELLONE

BREAKFAST CAKE

Ciambellone is one of the few puddings I associate with my nonna Tina. She wasn't particularly good at baking, and her cakes often turned out to be rather dense. These would then be eaten for breakfast and dunked in plenty of milk.

My mother usually made ciambellone when there was nothing else for breakfast in the house, because we always had flour, eggs, and sugar in the store cupboard. So, for us, Ciambellone—a really simple but moist cake, at least when my mother baked it—was inevitably associated with breakfast.

Serves 8
Preparation: 10 min
Baking time: 45 min

INGREDIENTS

300 g (2½ cups) plain
(all-purpose) flour
1 sachet (15 g / 3 tsp)
baking powder
1 pinch salt
4 medium eggs,
at room temperature
250 g (1¼ cups) caster sugar
(superfine sugar)
Seeds from 1 vanilla pod
Zest of 1 orange
165 ml (¾ cups) sunflower oil or
melted butter)
100 ml (½ cup) whole milk, at
room temperature
30 g (¼ cup) icing (powdered)
sugar, for sprinkling

PREPARATION

Preheat the oven to 180°C/350°F (non-fan setting).

Sift the flour into a bowl and combine with the baking powder and salt. Set aside.

Cream the eggs with the sugar, vanilla seeds, and orange zest using an electric whisk. Slowly work in the oil, continuing to whisk on a high setting. Alternately, add the flour mixture and milk, mixing everything on a low setting until you have a smooth and creamy consistency.

Transfer this mixture into a greased ring mould with a diameter of 24 cm/ 9.5 inches.

Bake in the centre of the oven for about 45 minutes. If the cake is going too dark after about 20–25 minutes, lower the temperature to 170°C/338°F. In this case, the cooking time can be extended by 5–6 minutes.

The cake is ready when a tester can be inserted without any of the mixture sticking to it. Leave the cake to cool in the tin for 15 minutes, then turn it out onto a serving dish and leave to cool completely. Dust with icing sugar to serve.

PAN DI RAMERINO
ROSEMARY BUNS

Pan di ramerino is a traditional bread that is both sweet and savoury. Once again, this is a recipe that uses up leftovers. In the past, wood-fired ovens were used for baking, and these retained their heat for a long while. To make the most of this residual heat, the leftover dough from large Tuscan loaves was used to bake these small, sweet buns. I have adapted the recipe slightly by including egg and butter for added flavour, and these ingredients beautifully complement the fragrant rosemary and sweet sultanas.

Makes 20 buns
Preparation: 60 minutes
Resting time: 5 hrs
Baking time: 20 min

INGREDIENTS

For the dough starter
(or pre-ferment):
4 g (0.14 oz) fresh brewer's yeast
150 ml (⅔ cup) water, lukewarm
150 g (1 cup plus 1 tbsp)
Manitoba flour

300 g (10 oz) sultanas (raisins)
100 ml (½ cup) vin santo
(Italian dessert wine)
10 g (0.35 oz) rosemary leaves
180 ml (¾ cup) extra-virgin
olive oil

For the dough:
800 g (1.75 lbs) Manitoba flour
100 g (½ cup) caster
(superfine) sugar
20 g (1 tbsp) fine salt
5 g (0.18 oz) fresh brewer's yeast
355 ml (1½ cup) lukewarm water

For topping:
Extra-virgin olive oil
1 egg yolk, beaten

PREPARATION

To make the dough starter, dissolve the brewer's yeast in the lukewarm water in a medium bowl, then add the flour and mix roughly. Cover the bowl with a kitchen towel or clingfilm and leave to prove for 2 hours somewhere that is protected from the cold. After 2 hours, the starter should have a semi-liquid consistency with little bubbles.

In a bowl, pour the vin santo over the sultanas and add enough water until they are covered. Soak for 1 hour, then drain and squeeze out the liquid. Finely chop the rosemary, add it to a pan with the olive oil, and warm these ingredients over low heat. As soon as the rosemary begins to toast, turn off the heat. Leave to cool slightly.

To make the dough, combine the Manitoba flour, sugar, and salt in a shallow bowl and mix by hand.

Dissolve the yeast in the lukewarm water, and add this mixture to the bowl with the dough starter. Add the flour mixture and knead for 5 minutes to combine. Add the rosemary oil to the dough, and continue kneading until it has been completely absorbed. Add the drained sultanas (that you have squeezed out well), and work these into the dough.

Transfer the dough to a floured work surface and continue kneading for about 10 minutes, until it has a smooth and not too soft consistency. Put the dough in a bowl, cover with a cloth or clingfilm, and leave to prove for about 2 hours somewhere that is protected from the cold. The dough will not rise as much as before, but it should still be nice and light.

Preheat the oven to 190°C/375°F non-fan setting). Line a baking tray with baking paper.

Divide the dough into 12 portions, each weighing roughly 80 g (3 oz). Shape these into balls and place them on the prepared baking tray, ensuring that you leave sufficient space for each bun to rise. Cover with a kitchen towel and leave to prove for 1 hour.

After an hour, brush the little buns with olive oil and bake for 15 minutes. Remove from the oven, brush with egg yolk, then continue baking for 5 minutes. Remove from the oven and leave to cool on a wire rack before tucking in!

RICOTTA FICHI E MIELE
RICOTTA WITH FIGS AND HONEY

In the garden at Poggianella, there are five large fig trees close to the water. Whenever my father brought ham home, we would run to the fig trees with little baskets, which we lined with fig leaves before carefully placing freshly picked figs on top. The fruit would then be conveyed home to be eaten with the ham. Sweet figs and salty ham create a mesmerising sensation in your mouth. I also combine figs with ricotta, which is a classic cream cheese that is available all over Italy and is easy to make at home.

Serves 4
Preparation: 10 min
Cooking time: 5 min
Resting time: 1–2 hrs

INGREDIENTS

1 litre (4¼ cups) whole milk
½ lemon
12 ripe figs
4 tbsp honey

TIP

Don't throw away the whey! It is very nutritious and can be used, for example, to make a smoothie or bake bread (instead of water).

PREPARATION

To make the ricotta: Heat the milk in a medium saucepan to a temperature of 90°C/194°F. Meanwhile, squeeze the juice from the lemon half through a fine sieve into a small bowl. When the milk is hot, remove the pan from the heat and add the lemon juice. Stir for a few seconds using a balloon whisk, then cover with a lid.

The milk will now separate into curds and whey; you will be able to see crumbly white lumps floating in the liquid. After 5 minutes, break up the resulting curds with a wooden spoon or balloon whisk. Wait a couple more minutes.

Line a sieve with cheese cloth or a kitchen towel, and place it over a bowl.

Pour the entire contents of the pan into the sieve, collecting the whey in the bowl. Leave the resulting ricotta to drain for a few seconds. Tie the cloth containing the cheese into a bundle, place it in a bowl, and refrigerate for about 1–2 hours. The ricotta is ready as soon as it starts to set inside the cloth.

As soon as the ricotta is firm and chilled, prepare the figs by trimming and washing them carefully. Slice the figs into quarters and set aside. Scoop the ricotta onto a plate, position the quartered figs on top, and drizzle with the honey.

PESCHE DI PRATO
STUFFED "PEACHES" FROM PRATO

When visiting Prato, I like to get up early in the morning and go to the area around the cathedral to sit at a table in one of the fantastic pâtisseries, for which my home city is famous. I order a freshly prepared Pesche di Prato, a traditional pastry from Prato that is inspired by delicious peaches. The classic Florentine bright red liqueur, alchermes, goes particularly well with this fluffy pastry, which has a crisp, sugary exterior and a soft centre filled with crema pasticcera. This exquisite treat plays with different consistencies and flavours.

Serves 20
Preparation: 90 min
Baking time: 20 min
Resting time: 4 hrs

INGREDIENTS
For the dough starter
(or pre-ferment):
225 g (1⅔ cups plus 3 tbsp)
plain (all-purpose) flour
37 g (3 tbsp) caster
(superfine) sugar
30 g (2 tbsp) butter, softened
17 g (0.6 oz) fresh brewer's yeast
100 ml (½ cup) water

For the dough:
375 g (2¾ cups) Manitoba flour
70 g (⅓ cup plus 1 scant tbsp)
caster (superfine) sugar
40 g (2¾ tbsp) butter, softened
4 large eggs
30 g (1 oz) honey
10 g (heaping ½ tbsp) fine salt
Zest of ½ orange
Seeds from 1 vanilla pod

PREPARATION
First, prepare the dough starter: Put the flour, sugar, and butter in the bowl of an electric mixer. Crumble the brewer's yeast into the water in a small bowl, then add this to the dry ingredients. Knead on low with the dough hook attachment of your electric mixer until smooth. Shape the dough into a ball, cover with a cloth, and leave to prove in a warm place for 60–90 minutes. It should almost triple in volume.

At the end of the proving time, mix the dough starter with all the flour using the dough hook attachment on your electric mixer. Add the sugar, butter, eggs, honey, salt, orange zest, and vanilla seeds. Knead everything on low until the dough no longer slaps against the sides of the bowl. Only at this point should the electric mixer be set to a higher speed. Continue kneading with the dough hook until the dough is smooth and dry and comes away from the sides. Check the dough by pulling a small piece apart between your fingers; if it stretches rather than tears, it is ready.

Transfer the dough to a work surface and shape it by hand into a ball. Put it in a bowl that has been dusted with flour, cover with a tea towel, and leave to prove for about 60–90 minutes; it should increase in size to roughly 2–2.5 times its original volume.

Once the dough has finished proving, turn it out on a lightly floured work surface and divide it into 5 pieces, each weighing roughly 100 g (3.5 oz). Roll each of these into equal-size sausages, splitting each one into 8 (12-g/0.4-oz) pieces. Without adding any more flour to the work surface, shape each piece into a small ball.

Recipe continues on p. 208.

For the crema pasticcera
(pastry cream):
½ vanilla pod
500 ml (2 cups) whole milk
125 g (4 oz) egg yolk
(approx. 7 eggs)
140 g (⅔ cup) caster
(superfine) sugar
40 g (⅓ cup) cornflour
(cornstarch)

For the alchermes syrup:
500 ml (2 cups) water
600 g (3 cups) caster
(superfine) sugar
175 g (¾ cup) alchermes
(Italian liqueur)

Caster (superfine) sugar, to coat
Candied orange peel,
for decoration

TIP
These are best eaten on the
day they are made.

Place the balls on a lined baking tray with gaps of about 1.5 cm/0.5 inches, and press down to flatten them slightly. Leave to rest for 10 minutes, then press the balls down again so they end up hemispherical in shape. Cover the tray with a cloth, and leave the dough to rise for about 2 hours. The rounds should almost triple in volume.

Bake the half-spheres at 200°C/400°F (non-fan setting) for 6–7 minutes. When they have turned pale brown, remove them from the oven and leave to cool for 30 minutes.

Prepare the crema pasticcera as described on p. 182.

Prepare the alchermes syrup as described on p. 191.

Pierce the flat sides of each cooled half-sphere with the tip of a small knife. Insert your thumb into this slit to make it slightly larger, and dip each half-sphere in the syrup. When all the half-spheres have been soaked in syrup, use a piping bag to inject some crema pasticcera into the centre of each, then spread a bit more crema over the flat surface. Finally, join pairs of half-spheres together to make wholes. Roll both sides of each sphere in sugar. Decorate the Prato peaches with pieces of candied orange to look like stalks.

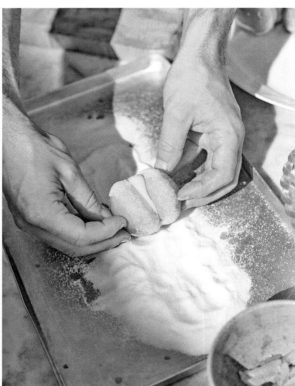

CASTAGNACCIO
CHESTNUT FLOUR CAKE

"What shall we eat today, kids?," asked Nonna Zita regularly, according to my mother. "Pane di legno, e vino del cielo" (bread made of wood and wine from the sky) was the joking response.

What they meant by "bread made of wood" was castagnaccio, which is made from chestnut flour, which comes from trees and thus from wood. There are lots of chestnut trees in the forests of Tuscany, which is why you find so many dishes that use chestnut flour in Tuscan cuisine. At a time when sugar was very scarce, this flour was a good choice because it has an inherent sweetness that is really welcome.

Chestnut flour was particularly prevalent during wartime, when there was a shortage of wheat flour. My father, Roberto, still remembers from his childhood how chestnut flour cakes would be made in the wood-fired oven, and how he would warm himself up by the oven with a piece of just-baked Castagnaccio in his hand.

Serves 16
Preparation: 15 min
Baking time: 30-40 min

INGREDIENTS
100 g (3.5 oz) sultanas (raisins)
600 g (5¼ cups) chestnut flour
800 ml (3⅓ cups) water
100 g (3.5 oz) walnuts
100 g (3.5 oz) pine nuts
Leaves from 1 sprig rosemary
3 g (½ tsp) fine salt
50 ml (3.5 tbsp) extra-virgin olive oil

PREPARATION
Wash the sultanas under running water, then soak them in a bowl of cold water for 15 minutes.

Sift the chestnut flour into a bowl and gradually add the water, stirring with a balloon whisk until you have a smooth, homogeneous mixture.

Set aside a few whole walnuts, pine nuts, and rosemary leaves to decorate the castagnaccio. Roughly chop the rest of the walnuts, finely chop the rosemary, and stir these into the mixture along with whole pine nuts.

Once the sultanas have finished soaking, squeeze out the liquid and add them to the batter, setting a few aside with the reserved pine nuts, walnuts, and rosemary for decoration. Add the salt to the batter and stir well.

Preheat the oven to 190°C/375°F (non-fan setting).

Grease a shallow, rectangular (40×25-cm/15.5×10.5-inch) cake tin with a little of the olive oil, pour in the batter, and smooth the surface. Sprinkle the reserved pine nuts, walnuts, and sultanas evenly over the surface of the cake. Finally, sprinkle the chopped rosemary and drizzle the remaining olive oil on top, then bake for about 30–40 minutes. Once cracks have appeared on the surface and the sultanas have developed a nice golden colour, remove the cake from the oven and leave to cool. The castagnaccio is ready to serve and enjoy.

MACEDONIA DI FRUTTA
FRUIT SALAD

La macedonia is a classic, simple fruit salad, and for me this is a real symbol of summer. It makes me think of the cooler evenings that follow hot days, and of spending time together, laughing and chatting. We often ate this for pudding at home; for special occasions, we added nuts and pine nuts. I like to make this with a dressing of oil and ginger, but it also goes brilliantly with ice cream.

Serves 8
Preparation: 20 minutes
Resting time: 20 minutes

INGREDIENTS
2 peaches
2 apples
½ cantaloupe melon
125 g (4 oz) strawberries
50 g (1.75 oz) blueberries
2 oranges
Zest of 1 lemon

For the dressing:
½ vanilla pod
2 tbsp extra-virgin olive oil
50 g (¼ cup) caster
(superfine) sugar
Juice of 1 lemon
½ tsp grated fresh ginger
6 mint leaves

To decorate:
6 mint leaves, chopped

PREPARATION

Carefully wash and dry the fruit. Slice the peaches in half and remove the stones. Chop the apples and peaches into segments, then cubes, and transfer to a large bowl. Halve the melon, remove the seeds, slice it into segments, then cubes, and add to the bowl. Halve the strawberries and them to the bowl, along with the blueberries.

Segment the oranges: First, cut the top and bottom off each orange so the flesh of the fruit is visible. Place the base on a chopping board, and use a knife to cut away the skin in strips from top to bottom, making sure you also completely remove the white pith, which has a bitter flavour. Cut between the membranes to release the individual orange segments. Hold the orange over a small bowl as you work to catch any juice that escapes. Add the orange segments to the bowl of fruit.

To make the dressing: Pour the juice from segmenting the oranges into a tall container. Scrape the seeds from the half vanilla pod into the container, and add the olive oil, sugar, lemon juice and zest, ginger, and mint leaves. Purée with a stick (emulsion) blender.

Pour the dressing over the prepared fruit and toss well. Cover and leave in the fridge for 20 minutes to allow the flavours to infuse. Scatter with the chopped mint just before serving.

TEAM

Mattia Risaliti (second from left) is a chef and food stylist from Berlin. He grew up in a large Tuscan family with 10 siblings. In chilly Berlin, he rediscovered a love of his native cuisine. Although the recipes made by his father, mother, and grandmothers had always been part of his life, it was only when he was in Germany—far away from Tuscany and its culinary specialities—that he really came to appreciate this food. His culinary creations are a way for him to indulge the people he cares about. He develops his own recipes, skilfully styling and showcasing his dishes for magazines and businesses.

Milia Seyppel (left) is a multiple award-winning designer from Berlin. She works as an interior designer, props stylist, and creative director, in addition to designing furniture and accessories that are sold internationally. She is passionate about illustration and artwork and is responsible for the graphic design of this book. Keeping the big picture in mind while having an eye for crucial details are key skills that she contributed to this project. She collected a veritable mountain of props for this book, which involved browsing at flea markets and hunting through the old closets of all her Italian relatives (especially on the lookout for tablecloths), unearthing items that were then used to good effect in the photos. She helped with the writing and with the translation into German.

Nathalie Mohadjer (third from left) is a prestigious photographer, who has lived for many years in Paris, where she works for internationally renowned magazines. Her natural style, along with an eye for lighting, imagery, and capturing the moment, makes her photography unmistakable and unique. Nathalie has an approach that puts anyone she photographs instantly at ease, so they emerge looking their best. Once she has a camera in her hand, there is no stopping her—she is relentless, grabbing every conceivable shot that could be useful to fill a 224-page cookbook, even as temperatures soared to 40 degrees C in the shade.

Dea Kaker (right) is an interior designer from Berlin. Her talents include creating wonderful interiors, designing furniture, producing ceramics on the side, and experimenting with delicious food. She regularly teams up with Mattia or works solo to make food for events and other projects. Without her assistance, there are several dishes here that would never have made it onto the plate.

GRAZIE

First of all, my deepest gratitude goes to my mother, Silvia, for always being there for me and for her unfailing support for all her children's interests. Thank you, Mamma, for your words and for your help with all the stories you told us, for spending hours going through our family recipes and photos. Thank you for the passion you bring to all your projects, something that you have passed on to me. Thank you for the belief you have in me and in all of us.

A special thank you must also go to my father, Roberto, for his support, for his enthusiasm about the Italian cuisine of his childhood, and for the stories he tells about this period. Thank you for cooking with me for this book, for allowing us to photograph you, for laughter at the dinner table, and all the kindness you have shown to me and my brothers and sisters.

Grazie to my siblings, Giovanni, Simone, Giacomo, Elisabetta, Maria Rachele, Stefano, Giuditta, Ester, Francesco, and Tommaso, all of whom have contributed to this book and have willingly allowed themselves to be filmed, who cooked with me and shared their own stories. I also owe thanks to all the partners of my siblings, Noemi, Paolo, Lorenzo, Silvia, Madda, Vittorio, Andrea, and Emma, and to my nieces and nephews, Sara, Martina, Gabriele, Matteo, Anna, Lisa, Marco, Pietro, Rebecca, Costanza, Diletta, Gregorio, Camilla, Filippo, Olivia, Martino, Agnese, Bernardo, Teresa, Gemma, Damiano, and Celeste. Thank you for playing your part, too, and for being part of this wonderful family together.

Grazie to everyone who helped us with various props: Nathalie and Elie, Giacomo and Noemi, William and Charlotte, Elisabetta and Paolo, Silvia and Stefano, Anka, Milia's grandfather Tony, and Barbara and Tombelli Ceramice.

Grazie to my mother-in-law, Sybille, for spending hours (to be honest it was days) proofreading and checking all the recipes. Thank you, Sybille, for listening, watching, coming up with ideas, and getting involved. Your support for us, whatever is happening in life, knows no limits and we are eternally grateful. There are doubtless recipes that would have been incomprehensible to the reader had it not been for your input.

Grazie to our friends who helped us out and came to Tuscany: Rohan and Isabel, Nathalie and Elie, William and Charlotte, Sep and Flo. You came from Berlin, Milan, Paris and Ghent, and we found ourselves all together in Tuscany again.

Grazie to my best friend, Dea, who always helps with my cooking projects and is a fantastic cook herself, flying out for 10 days to join us and help with the cooking. Without you, this book would never have been finished.

Grazie Clara and Piero, grazie Domenico, Elisabetta Pandolfini, Antonio Mattei, and Edoardo Pratesi for your contributions to this book.

Grazie to my son, Elio, for the love and chaos that you bring to our lives. Cooking with you is my absolute favourite activity—I love your crazy culinary experiments and the joy you take in them. At 3.5 years old, you are already a master chef.

Grazie Nathalie for your never-ending commitment that helped make this project a reality. Thank you for coming out with your entire family, for taking photos at 40°C despite a loose connection in the crucial cable, for your tireless, non-stop work and supreme commitment, for the constant quest for new stories and motifs for the book, for capturing all these special moments, for creating these wonderful photographs. I could never have dreamed they would be so beautiful. It was the greatest pleasure to have you as our family photographer because we regard you as one of us.

A special thank-you also goes to my darling wife, Milia, who was the first to believe in my crazy project and who offered unwavering support with the planning and implementation. The energy and determination you poured into this very long year of work was a constant inspiration to me and gave me the resolve to see the project through to the end. All the credit for the stunningly beautiful photography goes to you and is down to the dedication with which you worked on the design. I will never forget your quest for props in the attics and cellars of parents, friends, and grandparents, your discovery of family stories that would be so crucial for this book, the time you spent in numerous conversations with my family.

Thank you so much, Milia, for the many family memories that you sniffed out and brought to life so they could be included in these pages. These memories will live on and be treasured beyond this book. You are extraordinary and special, and that's why I love you.

INDEX

© Prestel Verlag, Munich · London · New York, 2024
part of Penguin Random House Verlagsgruppe GmbH
Neumarkter Straße 28 · 81673 Munich

© Text: Mattia Risaliti and Milia Seyppel, 2024
© Photography: Nathalie Mohadjer, 2024

Editorial direction: Claudia Stäuble
Project management: Veronika Brandt
Translation from German: Alison Tunley
Copyeditor: Peggy Paul Casella
Design: Milia Seyppel
Typesetting: Hilde Knauer, Cologne
Production management: Luisa Klose
Separations: Reproline Mediateam, München
Printing and binding: Livonia Print, Riga
Paper: Magno Natural

Penguin Random House Verlagsgruppe FSC® N001967

Printed in Latvia

ISBN 978-3-7913-8996-7

www.prestel.com

Elisabetta, Giovanni & Nonno Aimo, 1989

Nonno Aimo & noi, 1983

Nonni Romolo & Marisa con Mamma, 1958

Nonna Zita, 1978

Alla Poggianella 1989

Pulmino rosso, 1990